Electric RC Aircraft:
A Complete Resource

By
DVG Concepts

All rights Reserved 2013 DVG Concepts

Also By

DVG Concepts

Simplify – Making Life Simpler
Hurricane Preparation & Survival
RC Helicopters for Beginners
How Can I Make a Difference?
Why Can't I Get a Job?
Why Did I Fail? – Simple Steps for Turning Failure into Success!

Also by DVG Concepts, the How-To Mastery Series

RC Electric Cars
You Encourage Success!
How NOT to Suck at Management!

To my family who make
hobbies and everything else
much more fun

Contents

Introduction	6
Why an Electric Aircraft?	8
Technological Advances	17
Batteries	25
Electric Motors	43
How Many Channels Do You Need?	53
Control Systems	57
Sound Systems	64
Flight Simulators	66
RTF, ARF, or Kits?	71
Micro Aircraft	78
Where & What to Buy???	83
Wing Configuration	86
Pre-Flight Procedures	89
The Golden Rule	95
Flying Etiquette	100
Cleared for Take Off!	105
Flying Your RC Aircraft!	112
The Perfect Landing!	124
Learning How to Fly Your Helicopter	131
Avoiding a Crash!	136
When You Crash!	142
Conclusion	146
FREE R/C Hobby Information!	149

Disclaimer

The information contained in this publication is meant for educational purposes and for entertainment purposes only. It is intended to be used as a guide only and not a definitive resource for all applications and situations. It is the responsibility of the reader to ascertain which information is suitable and applicable for any and all situations. The writers, publishers and distributors assume no liability or responsibility for the use or application of any or all parts of this book. In other words, please use common sense and think before acting.

Why an Electric Aircraft?

It used to be that if you wanted to fly a remote control plane, you had to purchase a gasoline or nitro-fuel engine model. Along with this came the fuel, the glow plugs, the wiring the batteries and the manual starting of a motor that took many a chunk of skin of a not that quick finger.

Then came the first electric powered models but those were very expensive, very heavy, and the flight time was pretty darn poor. In reality, they were no real competition to the gas powered models and some of them were thought of as toys. Those that were not toys didn't replace the pilots gas planes; they merely were an addition more out of curiosity or status than anything else.

But then technology changed and so did the electric aircraft. As time went on, technology allowed batteries to hold more power in smaller and lighter packages and electronic technology made the electronics smaller, lighter and more efficient as well.

The result was longer flight time and lower prices. But flight times were still less than the gasoline models who still reigned as king.

But technology continued to improve and batteries got even smaller, lighter and more powerful while electronics became even lighter and more efficient. There were more features, more options and then, finally, motors were the last beneficiary of new technology.

With the new brushless motors, flight times went up to rival some of the gas powered models and the efficiency of those motors, along with increased power made full featured aircraft not only possible, but affordable. Now some of the long term gas aircraft fliers are turning to electric aircraft for their simplicity, ease of operation and convenience.

It used to be that electric aircraft, and their owners, were looked down upon at the local flight strip. Now, with more electric planes out there every year, the tide has changed. Electrics are more accepted, there are more models and options available and more stores and websites carry them than ever before. They are no longer considered toys; they are real life fully functional RC aircraft!

Electric aircraft are gaining popularity because of several factors and characteristics. Here are some of the advantages of electric aircraft over their gas powered counterparts:

Everything has the ability to fail at some point. When the thing that fails is sitting within inches of a half pint of highly flammable fuel, well, that never turns out well. Hence the fire extinguisher mentioned earlier.

Also, internal combustion engines generate heat. A lot of heat. The air flow during flight helps keep them cool but they still will get hot. If you are not careful, parts of the engine can burn you if you touch them. With that in mind, you might want to add a first aid kit to the list of items above. (It's a good idea for electrics as well just as a precaution as both models have spinning propellers…..)

Electric motors do not generate nearly as much heat although they will get warm as they operate. But when an electric motor fails, it usually just stops. While it could overheat and catch fire, that is rare as there are usually fuses and safety circuits built into the motor or the controller to keep that from happening.

Lastly, think about this: when you start a gas engine, you are right there and your fingers are really, really right there. When you start an electric aircraft, you can be as far away as you want when you move that joystick. If you have kids nearby, this can be a big comfort for you.

Are we exaggerating the dangers of operating a gas aircraft? Probably. After all they have been around for a long time and they have a pretty good track record. But when you compare them to operating electric aircraft, electrics are just much safer. While you are not likely to lose an arm or leg with either one but your fingers will be safer with the electrics!

Electrics Are Cleaner & More Environmentally Friendly

Gas engines have exhaust gases. Contained in those exhaust gases are the by-products of the combustion process plus the remnants of the lubrication additives that are contained within the fuel that lubricate the engine surface so they do not overheat and seize.

Anyone who has flown a gas engine plane, car or helicopter understands what we are talking about. Having to wipe down the entire airplane body after applying glass cleaner to get off the sticky oil residue is a ritual after every day of flying. There is none of that with an electric aircraft.

I am not sure how damaging the exhaust gases are to the environment but let's just say this. There are no emissions or gases from an electric aircraft. I guess if you really push it, the power plants that generate the electricity to charge the battery might emit some gases but do you really want to go that far? If you do, then let's talk about the manufacturing of the fuel and the plastic used in the fuel bottles and the spillage and the throwing out of old fuel that is no longer good. Just admit it. Electric aircraft are cleaner.

Electrics Are Cheaper to Fly

OK, this might be subject to debate. Electrics do not use fuel so you don't have to purchase fuel, replace glow plugs and buy starting batteries.

But electrics do use rechargeable batteries and batteries have to be replaced eventually, so that offsets some of the fuel costs. I still think there are more expenses with gas engines and we'll get to more of those expenses in a just a minute.

Electrics Require Less Maintenance & Upkeep

Gas engines have more moving parts and they generate heat and put out sticky emissions and they require glow plugs. All of these things are maintenance issues. Glow plugs burn out and need to be replaced, engines wear out or get dirty and need to be cleaned and adjusted. All of those things take time.

Cleaning the body of the residue of exhaust gases is tedious and every so often you really have to get in deep and clean everything or moving surfaces get gummed up. Gas motors also have more vibration and that takes its toll on motor mounting screws and bolts. They have to be tightened and checked regularly as well as servo screws and other fasteners. Vibration causes things to loosen up over time.

There will be fuel lines to replace every so often as the age or crack as well. Everything considered, gas planes are more maintenance intensive. Electrics have little maintenance and little to go wrong. Yes you have to do your preflight checks and go over the aircraft for loose screws and bolts but you won't find that many.

Electrics Are Quieter

Some electrics are so quiet you will have to look at them to make sure the propeller is turning. Gas engines, on the other hand, can sound like a cat caught in a fan belt. Some pilots love the sound and it is more realistic but you can fly an electric next door while you neighbor is sleeping and no one will care!

Part of flying is being a good neighbor and some people are not thrilled with listening to a gas engine whine and whine. In fact, the noise might keep you from flying on many fields and parks. Anywhere with noise restrictions is not a place where a gas engine aircraft flier is going to feel welcome.

Electrics Can Re-Start in-Flight

Here is something that most people might not even think about. If a gas engine stops in mid-flight for some reason, it is not easy to restart. Sometimes it is impossible. The engine might stall because of a maneuver keeping fuel from the engine or for some other reason. When that happens, the technical term often used is that the pilot is "screwed". As I said, that is an aircraft technical term.

But if an electric motor should stop, reapplying power to it should make it start right up unless the battery is discharged or the motor itself defective. This can enable you to re-gain control of the aircraft and correct any flight condition that caused the original problem.

This might not happen often but it only has to happen once for you to be thankful for the ability to re-start!

Electrics are Easier to Store and Transport

Gas or Nitro-fuel has to be stored and transported to the flight area. This stuff is extremely flammable and you do not want to store it inside your home or apartment. You don't even want it in the car with you and you need to secure it while it is sitting in the trunk.

Leftover fuel from one year of flying may go bad before next year and that fuel has to be disposed of properly as well. On the other hand, a battery that has reached the end of its life can be recycled at the local library or recycling center.

Technological Advances

Over time, people look for ways to make things better. To solve major and critical life events. They strive to find objectives to make things better, to solve life's problems and to improve our quality of life. Advances in medical research have brought us CAT scans and MRI tests and a host of other improvements that enable us to live longer and also to live with a higher quality of life.

So you might be wondering now, what does this have to do with remote control aircraft?

The answer is simpler than one might realize. Whenever new technology is developed for something, that same technology "trickles down" to other applications as well. If a company creates a way to make electronic circuits smaller so that a better pacemaker can be made smaller, that is great news.

But that same technology can also result in making hearing aids smaller and portable sound equipment made smaller and better as well.

The companies that manufacture or design remote control equipment also get word of this new technology and they bring it to the world of RC flying.

People also want something newer and better to replace what they already have. Or they want something with more features. Last, but certainly not least, they want to see more of the higher end technology made affordable.

So let's look at what technology has done for the world of model RC planes and helicopters:

Lighter

Technology has brought us new materials and advancements that allow us to make aircraft and helicopters that weight just a fraction of what they weighed just a few years ago.

Electronics are now so much lighter that we can reduce the weight of the aircraft and make it more responsive and agile. We can also pack in more features and controls as well.

Smaller

New compounds and technology has made it possible to produce airplanes and helicopters at a fraction of the size of models made just 10 years ago. We now have model RC planes that can fly in your living room and do not have to have huge outside areas in which to enjoy the flying experience.

That means people in the city can enjoy flying just like the people in the suburbs. Helicopters that take off and land in your hand are now available at really low prices. This not only makes the hobby more accessible, it makes it easier and therefore more fun as well.

Longer Flight Time

With the arrival of more efficient motors and controllers and more powerful batteries, flight time now rivals some of the better gasoline or nitro powered models. Gone are the days of the 5 minute electric flight. The combination of the newer brushless motors and more efficient electronics allow us to get more time from our systems and batteries. As we all know, more time equals more fun.

More Features

Today we have more channels and more features and controls than ever before. Anti-crash circuitry and even sound systems to produce real aircraft engine sounds are all possible due to new and improved technology.

Do you need all of these things? Probably not but if something is available and you think it is really cool, why not get it? The purpose of this hobby is to have as much fun as possible. If technology allows us to do something, and we want to do it, we should go for it and put a smile on our faces!

Longer Range

The range over which we can fly our aircraft is important. If something has only a 100 foot range, we will just be able to fly in a circle all day long. That is not much fun! But with advances in electronics we are able to make more powerful transmitters and more sensitive receivers.

This means our aircraft can fly longer and more accurately without the fear of losing control because of limited range. Transmitters now operate in higher frequencies meaning lower losses and even more range. All of this helps make flying more fun and much more safe for everyone.

More Reliable

If you are an old timer, then you might remember the old tube type televisions. If you are younger, go ask your grandfather! These tube type receivers used vacuum tubes to process all the signals needed to reproduce your television picture. They did the job but they were always burning out or weakening. Repairmen made a fortune replacing tubes every few months or so. Now we have flat panel televisions with nothing to wear out and they work for years with no maintenance except wiping them with a rag to remove dust and dirt.

RC aircraft are the same way. Old unreliable mechanical systems are now replaced with totally electronic systems which not only use less power but are maintenance free and last a long time.

Newer batteries (we'll get to those next chapter) are more reliable and don't leak all over damaging the airplane or copter in the process. Even factors like heat and moisture no longer have much of an effect on today's parts and pieces because of different manufacturing and materials.

Lower Cost

10 years ago I bought a trainer airplane and transmitter and it cost me about $400. Today, I can get a better and bigger plane with more range and more flying time for about half of that amount. This is because technology has lowered the cost of manufacturing these aircraft and making them more affordable.

For those who remember (ask grandpa again if you have to) the first color TV's were huge things that required two men to lift them and they cost about $700 for a 19 or 21 inch screen. Today you can get a state of the art 60" television for that price. The picture is much better, it is more reliable and one person can lift or move it.

More Features

Sometimes technology doesn't give us lower prices but helps provide us with more features. When it comes to RC aircraft, we have increased control, fail safe technology and anti crash systems. We have the ability to control lights and have greater and more accurate control over the aircraft and what it can do. All because of technology.

Upgrades

With everything being made smaller and lighter, there is a greater chance for upgrading your older plane than ever before. While it is sometimes difficult to replace something with something else that is heavier or bulkier, going better, lighter and smaller is usually not much of a problem. It is always easier to add a little weight to balance off the new part than it is to balance a plane because you used a bigger battery or bulkier motor.

Manufacturers realize there is a huge upgrade and improvement market out there and will make a lot of retrofit kits out there to help everyone make their planes better, faster or fly longer.

The Future of Technology for RC Aircraft

When I say the sky's the limit, I am not trying to be funny. But think about what we have today and what you might have though impossible just 25 years ago. In 1985 if someone would have told you that you could rent a movie from a kiosk for $1.50 a day whenever you wanted you would have thought they were crazy! When movies first came out on video tape they were $100 now they are less than 10 buck in high def no less!

The GPS you use to find out how to get where you were going would have been just a dream years ago. The same for the high capacity hard drives we have today. (My first computer was ordered with a high capacity hard drive that was a whopping 150MB! Today we have Terabyte drives that we take for granted.

So the future of RC aircraft as a hobby is open ended. Automatic take offs and landing, pre-programmed flights; added features and even solar power to keep the plane or copter up in the air all day are possibilities.

We are already seeing video cameras for planes and copters and you can be sure that will be improved as well over time. The only thing right now that is definite is that whatever you buy today will be improved upon tomorrow. Things will only get better, smaller and lighter.

But the one important thing to remember is that as long as your plane can still fly, you can have a ton of fun with it. Just like people continue to drive vintage cars, that plane that you have had for years will still provide you with hours of excitement and enjoyment. There is no need to trade it is or retire it as long as it makes you happy.

Batteries

While you don't need to be an engineer to fly an RC aircraft, or even to plug a battery in, there are still a few things you should know about the batteries you use and how they operate. This will help you make the right choices and get the most enjoyment out of your RC aircraft.

First, let me say one very important thing regarding batteries. When they are used and stored in the proper manner batteries today are very safe and are not likely to cause any problems. But if you don't take care of them and use them properly, they can explode or catch fire and cause injury to people and damage to your home and aircraft. That does not mean you need to be fearful of your batteries, only that you need to pay attention to some very simple facts.

Battery Types

When we usually think of batteries we think of flashlight batteries and AA, AAA, C and D batteries. In fact, we use some of those sizes in our transmitters.

But the batteries that are used on board the aircraft are usually some type of rechargeable battery. We will start with those first.

Rechargeable batteries can be recharged after they are "dead" or become discharged. Instead of throwing them away, you plug them into a charger designed for rechargeable batteries and wait for a certain period of time for the battery to regain its charge.

These chargers should not be confused with the old battery chargers that claimed to recharge standard batteries. Those really just prolonged the life of the battery and each time they were supposedly "recharged" they held less and less of a charge and eventually just died a slow and agonizing death.

Instead, true rechargeable batteries can be brought back to a full charge within a few hours. The level of charge will degrade slowly over time but for the most part, they will continue to regain a full charge for quite a while.

There are 3 main types of rechargeable batteries on the market for RC aircraft today. Those are Nickel Cadmium or "NI-CAD's" batteries, Lithium-ION batteries and LIPO or Lithium Polymer batteries. These represent the oldest (NI-CAD's) to the newest (LIPO) battery technologies available today. Tomorrow there will undoubtedly be something new but for now, these are the 3 you should know about and understand.

Nickel-Cadmium Batteries

These batteries have been around for years. They were among the first true rechargeable batteries and have been used in all sorts of applications for years and years. They are very durable and have proven themselves on jobsites and rough use applications for a long time as well. They are time tested and safe to operate. The voltage per cell in a NI-CAD is 1.2 volts which will become important to you shortly.

The disadvantages of NI-CAD batteries are their size and weight and the amount of power they deliver per pound. NI-CADs deliver the least amount of power per pound of the 3 battery types. They also have some of what is commonly referred to as a "memory effect".

Memory effect is when a battery does not take a full charge unless it is usually taken down to "empty" before recharging. If you take a NI-CAD and always recharge it when it is only half empty, eventually it will only give you partial performance. Sometimes you can completely discharge the battery and charge it several times to restore performance but sometimes this is permanent.

So if you own some NI-CAD batteries, it is a good idea to drain them almost completely before recharging them. This will minimize the memory effect and make the batteries perform better and last longer. It should also be mentioned that NI-CADs have a higher self discharge rate than the other 2 batteries.

Self discharge means the amount of charge the battery loses by just sitting over time with nothing hooked up to it. A NI-CAD can lose all of its charge in a couple of months, possibly shorter.

Another disadvantage of NI-CAD's is that they are made with cadmium which is a heavy metal and not good for the environment. We wouldn't be surprised to see NI-CADs phased out because of this factor alone.

Lithium-Ion Batteries

Technology brought us a better rechargeable battery because the weight of NI-CAD batteries made them impractical for some applications such as electric vehicles. Those batteries were so bulky and so heavy they just were not an acceptable solution. So scientists and engineers got together and gave us the Lithium-Ion battery.

Lithium-Ion batteries are much lighter than NI-CADs and they can pack a lot more power into a smaller and lighter footprint than a NI-CAD can. This means not only do they weigh less but you can put more of them in the same amount of space compared to NI-CADs. They can be made very thin which allows them to fit places NI-CADs couldn't.

The cell voltage of a Lithium-Ion battery is approx 3.6 volts which also means fewer cells are needed to create higher voltages. But remember the cell voltage because it will become important later on.

Lithium-Ion also has almost no self discharge which means it will retain almost all of its charge for long period of time. This makes it very valuable for devices which use little power but are located in areas where changing or charging a battery is inconvenient. The low self discharge also makes for a more energy efficient use as less charging is required over time.

Lithium-Ion batteries also have little or no memory effect. You can recharge as often as you like whether the battery is completely empty or almost full without damaging the battery or affecting it performance. (I still prefer to deep discharge my batteries before charging but that's just the "old school" engineer in me!)

Lithium-Ion batteries were a huge benefit to model RC aircraft because not only were the batteries lighter and smaller but they provided more power as well. More power equals more run time and more run time means longer flight times. And we all know longer flight time means more fun on flight day.

The disadvantage of lithium-ion batteries is that they are more prone to heat issues and they are more expensive than NI-CAD's. They also may have shipping restrictions on them because of the chemicals used to manufacture them.

Lithium Polymer Batteries

Lithium Polymer batteries, or LI-PO's as they are known are the latest battery technology as of the writing of this book.

That will undoubtedly change as technology changes but for now, LI-PO's are the state of the art battery.

LI-PO's are similar to lithium Ion batteries in that they hold more power in a lighter and smaller package than NI-CAD's. This means they can be used to power smaller, lighter and more compact aircraft. If you have seen the really small hand held helicopters and micro-planes then you are probably looking at LI-PO batteries inside those designs.

Another advantage to a LI-PO is that they can be made very thin and in a lot of different shapes. So they can be designed to fit just about anywhere. They pack quite a power punch and there is no memory effect and very little self-discharge.

The LI-PO battery is also naturally the most expensive being the latest technology and having the most desirable characteristics. But LI-PO's are not all that expensive and they do not inflate the cost of aircraft using them.

Non-Rechargeable Batteries

Some transmitters will not use rechargeable batteries. They might come with, or call for standard Alkaline AA or AAA batteries. These batteries are not rechargeable and you will have to replace them when they run down. There are a few things everyone needs to know about non rechargeable versus rechargeable standard size batteries.

First, the voltage for a standard size AAA or AA battery is 1.5 volts. If you purchase a rechargeable AAA or AA battery it will likely be a NI-CAD and their voltage is 1.2 volts. While .3 volts is not a lot, it adds up when you have 6 or 8 of them in your transmitter. For example, if you have 8 batteries in your transmitter, with standard batters that is 8 X 1.5 or 12 volts. If you use rechargeable batteries then that becomes 8 X 1.2 which is 9.6 volts. That is a big difference. Fortunately most transmitters are designed to readily accept both type of batteries and their circuitry is designed to operate on both types.

Second, regular batteries will lower their voltage as they run down. Rechargeable batteries tend to keep working until almost the end and then they just quit. Regular batteries will run down more gradually. So if you are using regular batteries in the transmitter and you notice sluggish operation or reduced range, land the aircraft immediately because the batteries are going dead.

If you use standard batteries you should ALWAYS use alkaline batteries. They are more powerful and the technology is far better. Do not use cheap non alkaline batteries for any reason on your RC equipment. There is just too much at stake to lose. Always purchase name brand batteries and stay away from discount store or store brand batteries.

Battery Brands

There are a lot of options and alternatives to buying batteries from the manufacturers.

But if you decide to purchase an aftermarket battery, there are some things you need to be aware of.

First, just because a battery has LI-PO stamped on it does not guarantee the battery is, in fact, a LI-PO battery. I can print anything on the case of the battery and call it whatever I want. You might be getting a LI-PO and you might be getting a Lithium-Ion. You might even be getting a NI-CAD and you'll never know. This could be dangerous for reasons you will still learn but just be careful.

Second, just like you cannot be sure you are getting the type of battery it says it is, you might not be getting a battery with the power that is stamped on it either. Manufacturers can play games with how they rate their battery and just like battery type; they can stamp anything they want on the battery. Just because it says so does not make it true.

Third, battery brands are important if you should ever require service or have to return a battery. If you purchase a reputable battery like a Duracell or Eveready, there are places you can go to return the battery if it is defective or even to get reimbursed if their battery damages a piece of equipment. If you bought your battery on some off brand website or EBAY, you might be out of luck. Also, name brand batteries are far more likely to be what they say they are as far as type and power.

When it comes to batteries, do not be cheap. Having a $500 aircraft flying 200 feet up when your transmitter has some of those "20 for $1" batteries is just asking for trouble.

Purchase high quality, name brand batteries so they will not just quit working and you watch your plane fly off into the sunset or plummet to the earth!

Battery Chargers

OK, here is something you really need to know and understand. You should ALWAYS use the charger that came with the battery. If you purchase replacement or second batteries, you MUST only charge them with the same charger that you use on the other same type batteries. If you fail to follow this simple rule you could cause your battery to catch fire or explode! Here's why.

Remember when we mentioned the voltages of some of the different type of batteries? We said the NI-CAD voltage per cell was 1.2 but the per cell voltage of both lithium based batteries was 3.6. If you try to charge your NI-CAD with a lithium charger or vice versa, you will either not be able to charge the battery or you will damage it or worse.

The battery voltage is important as well when it comes to charging. All batteries combine several cells in one package to get higher voltage. For example a 4.8 volt NI-CAD has 4 cells in the one package. In order to charge this battery you would need a 4.8 volt charger. All chargers are different and have different voltage outputs. You cannot charge a 4.8 volt battery with a 12 volt charger even if the connector is the same!

I suggest everyone do two things when they get their aircraft. First write on the battery and the charger which goes with which. This will eliminate confusion later on when you have more than one aircraft or battery. Label all replacement batteries as well. Also write on each battery the time it takes to fully charge that battery. This will help you when it comes to getting ready for the next flight day.

If batteries should start to get hot during recharging, check to make sure you are using the correct charger. If you are, it might be that the battery is approaching the end of its useful life and that something has changed within it. While it is acceptable and normal for batteries to get warm during recharging, they should not get really hot. Eventually you will get a "feel" for what is normal. If a battery gets warmer than normal, then look into getting a replacement.

Battery chargers carry ratings for both voltage and current. Voltage needs to match the battery and you should never use a charger with a different voltage rating than what the battery requires. Current ratings indicate how much power the charger can put out. A charger with a higher current rating may allow the battery to charger faster. Using a lower current charger than specified can make the battery take a lot longer to fully charge.

Battery Ratings

Batteries are usually rated in terms of both voltage and current.

Rechargeable batteries will often use both ratings while standard batteries will usually just use voltage.

For example, AAA, AA, C and D batteries are all 1.5 volts. Voltage is important because it needs to match the voltage needs of the equipment in order for everything to function properly. Equipment can be damaged by using a higher voltage battery. Components can get burned out if this is done. Using a lower voltage battery may cause damage as well but usually the result is just that the device will not operate properly or at all.

The current rating is how much power the battery can deliver. The higher the number the more power the battery can deliver. Since higher power means longer flight time, more is good! Current is usually listed in milliamps (ma) or amps (A). A milliamp is one one-thousandth of an amp.

You might see a rating called "peak or instantaneous power" and this is the amount of power the battery can deliver for a very short period of time under a heavy load. This is almost meaningless and you should always make sure the power rating of a battery is accurate and not misstated.

For those of you not familiar with electricity and things like voltage and current, here is a short explanation.

Voltage

Voltage is the "force" or pressure behind the electricity.

The higher the voltage, the more force or "push" it will have. You can generate more power and more torque from a higher voltage motor. With batteries you increase the voltage by adding more cells inside the battery or using more than one battery.

Current

The current, usually measure in milliamps or amps, is the amount of electricity that can be delivered. Current is more like volume. Think of current like water flowing through a pipe. If the force behind the water is the same, you will get a lot more water through a 10 inch pipe than you would through a 1 inch pipe. The higher the current capacity the more power the battery will be able to produce.

Connectors

Some batteries will fit into a holder or case with wires connecting it to the device it is going to power. Other batteries simply plug in through a connector at the end of a wire attached to the battery. Either way works just fine it is a matter of design only.

One thing you need to understand is just because a battery connector will fit into a device does NOT mean the battery is the right one. Also, just because a battery attaches to a charger does not mean the two are compatible. You must always check to make sure that you are attaching the battery to the right device.

There are no standard connectors or reasons for using a specific connector. So make sure both device and battery are labeled to make sure you correctly pair the two before connecting!

When You Get a New Battery

By now you are somewhat of an expert on batteries. You know the different types and you know which ones are best and why. You also know about the need to use the correct charger that matches the type battery you are using. If you don't know these things PLEASE go back and re-read this chapter. It is that important.

But it is also important to understand that not all batteries are alike. Just because they look the same and have the same things printed on them does not make them equal. Since flying time is very dependent on the battery used, we should always test new batteries first to make sure they will perform as expected.

You should let the aircraft run for a while to see if the battery will power the aircraft for the expected period of time. If you own a helicopter this is easy because you can just hover the helicopter a few inches high and measure how long the battery lasts. For aircraft this can be more difficult since flying low can be dangerous. You might just want to run the propeller to see how long it will run but this can be dangerous as well since the electric motors sometimes use the air flow moving past them in flight to keep them cool.

One test you might consider is attaching a light bulb (the same voltage as the battery) or some other device (again using the same voltage) and measuring how long the battery powers that device. If you standard or original battery powers the device or bulb for the same time as the new one, you are good to go. If the new battery performs longer that's even better. But if the new battery only powers it for half the time, you better be aware of that and adjust your flight time accordingly.

Since some batteries look alike, I always like to write down the date that the battery was purchased on the battery in permanent magic marker. This allows you to tell the batteries apart and to always know which ones are the newest and freshest. This also holds true for the standard batteries used in your transmitter.

I never allow the batteries in my transmitter to go dead or even get close to becoming discharged. I will put in a new set and then use the old ones in flashlights or other devices where it is not a big deal if they go dead. It just helps protect my investment.

Battery Aging

Batteries do age like a lot of other things in life. For rechargeable batteries the first indication of aging is taking a longer time to charge and a reduced flight time. This is because the chemicals in any battery change over time.

For rechargeable batteries, you can recharge those thousands of times and that is what makes them so desirable. But as they get older they will start lasting less and less. When you notice this, it is time to plan on replacing the battery or at least having fresh ones available in case the battery fails all together.

It is good practice to keep your rechargeable batteries charged even when you are not using them. NI-CADs will lose their charge sitting on the shelf so those will require more attention. Lithium based batteries will not lose much of their charge so this is not much of an issue.

Even though lithium batteries do not have much of a memory effect, I still like depleting the battery almost to empty before recharging. This is strictly a personal choice and is probably because I have grown up with the older style batteries. But it makes sense to me and it surely doesn't do the battery any harm.

That being said, it is ever a good idea to totally drain down any rechargeable battery to the point where there is no charge left. If you do have to do that, recharge it promptly. Never let a rechargeable sit dead for long period of time.

Battery Disposal

Part of being a good RC hobbyist is being aware of the environment and recycling whenever possible. When it comes to batteries, you should not be disposing of any battery directly into the garbage.

Whenever possible take all kinds of batteries to your local recycling center or to a battery disposal bin. You might find them at your local library or even a local supermarket.

Batteries, especially NI-CAD's contain chemicals that are very harmful to the soil and to the air if burned or incinerated. So putting them in the garbage will allow them to wind up in a land fill or in garbage incinerator and neither of those are good.

Speaking of incinerators, placing any kind of battery in a fire of any kind is one first class bad idea. Batteries can explode and cause serious injury to those around when they do. Always dispose of batteries in the proper manner. It is a small price to pay for enjoying your RC aircraft.

Battery Care

Batteries today are pretty much maintenance free. But that does not mean you don't have to properly care for them. Here are a few things you should keep in mind when it comes to your batteries:

Avoid Hot and Cold

Keep your batteries away from extreme hot or cold. Heat can damage the battery and freezing can damage the chemicals inside the battery and crack the case causing batteries to leak. Also, avoid flying in very cold weather as many batteries will have their power capabilities reduced in very cold weather. In those times flight times will be much lower.

Remove Dead or Discharged Batteries

Dead or discharged batteries, especially standard or alkaline batteries are prone to leakage as they get older. Batteries do have a shelf life and they should never be used past that shelf life. The chemicals that leak out are very acidic and will destroy the connections and equipment they are installed in.

Remove Batteries When Not in Use

Because of the above, it is good practice to remove the batteries from all equipment at the end of flying season if there is one in your area. Remove them from your aircraft and transmitters so they do not have a chance to do any damage during the winter. This is especially true if you store your aircraft outside.

Keep the batteries inside in a protected are where they will not be subjected to heat and cold.

Keep Batteries Dry

Water and batteries do not mix very well. Keep your batteries safe and dry to get the most use out of them. Keeping them in a closed plastic box will help not only keep them dry and safe but keep them organized as well.

Charging Your Batteries

Follow the manufacturer's directions on how to charge the batteries.

Charge them fully but do not leave them on charge all the time. Not only is this a waste of energy, it is not good for the charger or battery either.

Keep you batteries charged and remove them from the charger once they become fully charger. You can keep a log of when the battery was last charged as well so you will have a good idea when or if it needs to be recharged.

Electric Motors

Electric motors are the heart of any RC electric aircraft. The motor is what powers the aircraft and makes flight possible. Without the motor, our helicopter couldn't fly and our airplane would have to be content with becoming a glider.

Technology has made a huge difference in the motors we now use to power RC aircraft. Though some of the old tried and true motors are still being used, more and more we are going to the new technology to enable our aircraft to be smaller, lighter and fly further and further.

There are two basic forms of electric motors. While you do not need to be an engineer or understand how exactly these motors work, you should understand the characteristics of each type so you can make an intelligent decision when it comes time for you to purchase your next aircraft.

The two type of motors are brush-type and brushless. As the name implies, one motor uses brushes and the other doesn't.

But there are more differences than that so let's get into why brushless motors are the best option now and will likely still be in the future.

Brush Type Motors

Brush type motors have been around for decades and decades. If you owned any toy or model over the past 50 years it probably had a brush type motor inside powering the toy. These are simple type motors with a permanent magnet on the outside and a rotating coils wound on a metal base on the inside.

The coil is connected to a device called a **commutator** whose purpose is to constantly change the direction of electricity flowing through the coils. This made the coils alternated being attracted to the permanent magnets and then repelled by those same magnets. The result was a rotating electromagnet that was connected to the shaft of the motor. The more voltage applied to the motor and the faster the motor would spin.

This was a very simple and effective design and it worked fairly well for a long time. But there were some problems with this design that caused it to fall out of favor with many manufacturers and RC users.

First of all, the brushes that rubbed against the commutator and carried the electricity to and from the motor would become worn over time. All the friction and movement would wear away from the surface of the brush.

The brushes were backed up by small springs that would push the brush forward as it wore down but eventually those brushes had to be replaced. Some motor designed made this difficult or impossible. The only option was motor replacement.

Another disadvantage was that this type of design was just not that efficient. There was a lot of energy wasted on heat and friction and this made performance suffer. The motors were often noisy as well. The faster the motor would spin, or the larger the motor, the noisier it would be and this created problems in some applications. As far as RC aircraft were concerned, however, they were still quieter than their gas engine counterparts.

But this design had another disadvantage when it came to RC aircraft. The brush and commutators created sparks during operation. While these sparks were small and not dangerous, they did create interference and electronic noise.

Electronic "noise" occurs whenever something creates an electrical field or signal and every time the brushes in the motor sparked, it created a small electrical signal. It was a type of static that normally you wouldn't hear or be concerned about but when you are controlling something 300 yards away with a radio transmitter, this type of noise was not always a good thing.

The noise could limit range and interfere with the control of the aircraft and this often created problems.

Transmitters and receivers had circuitry to minimize this type of problem but it was still something to be concerned about.

Controlling brush type motors was both easy but inefficient. To make the motor go faster or slower you just had to increase or decrease the voltage going to the motor.

But this was usually done with something called a rheostat and those parts wasted energy that wasn't being sent to the motor. What was needed was a more efficient way to of controlling the motor that would place less of a drain on the battery.

Hence the design and creation of the brushless motor.

Brushless Motors

Brushless motors do not use a commutator or any brushes. Hence the name brushless. (DUH!) Instead of the rotating electromagnet the brush type motor had, the rotating part of the brushless motor was a permanent magnet and the coils are stationary. Since there are no connections needed to transmit electricity to the moving parts of the motor, the brushes and commutator were no longer needed.

Brushless motors are much more efficient and they are quieter and deliver more torque than brush type motors do. This translates into using less energy from batteries and for RC pilots; this translates into longer flying time.

Since there are no brushes to wear down or replace maintenance is much less and the motors are much more reliable. This also eliminates the sparking and interference caused by the brushes. It is just an all around better design. Brushless motors can also be sealed off from dirt and dust which further increases their reliability. So not only do brushless motors perform better and more efficiently, they have almost no interference and that is a welcome effect for RC flyers as well.

Brushless motors are controlled by devices called controllers (again, DUH!). These controllers make the motor go faster and slower according to the need at the time. These controllers are much more efficient than brush type controller and this gives even more power savings which also translates into longer flight time.

There are two basic types of brushless motors. They are called **in runner** and **out runner** motors. In runner motors have their magnets rotating inside the coils and out runner models have their magnets rotating outside the coils. Not that you will even need to understand this, it is just good to know. In runner motors are the most common for RC aircraft while out runner motors allow for more torques at lower RPM (revolutions per minute). This might allow for larger propellers to be powered directly without the gear for gear reduction.

Which Motor is Right for You?

Just because something is newer does not mean it is right for you or your application. If you currently have an aircraft with a brush type motor and you are just learning or are happy with it, just leave it be. There is absolutely nothing wrong with those motors. But if you are considering purchasing a newer aircraft, or your first aircraft, then you might wish to consider your options.

Brush type motors are the least expensive. So if you are just looking for the cheapest plane, then a brush type motor might be the best choice.

This is especially true if you are just starting out and not sure if this is for you. But if you have some experience and really think you will be in this for the long haul, base your decision not on what you need today but also your needs for tomorrow.

Motor Conversion

Maybe you already have an aircraft that you like but it has an older motor. Maybe your old motor has quit and requires replacement and the rest of the aircraft is still in good shape. If that is the case, you might wish to convert to a brushless motor.

Converting to a brushless motor is not as straightforward as you might think. You have to consider size and weight and overall balance of the aircraft. You will also need to replace the controller as well because the two motors usually have different type controllers.

The best choice would be if the aircraft manufacturer had a conversion kit or at least directions on how to proceed and recommended motors. But since that often is not the case, check with third party vendors to see if they have a kit. Lastly, your local RC aircraft dealer or hobby shop might be able to recommend something or someone to you.

Always keep in mind that changing any part of an aircraft involves careful planning and balancing of the aircraft. With a helicopter you might discover a problem a few inches off the ground.

But with an airplane, you might be 15-50 feet in the air before you notice. That could cause significant damage. If you are at all in doubt of your skills and abilities in this area I would suggest you hire someone to do the conversion or just go out and buy a new model with the motor you want. When you factor is time and labor for someone else to do a conversion, a new aircraft might be the best, and most economical, path to take.

Motor Maintenance

Brush type motors require maintenance to keep the brushes and commutator in good working order. If you particular motor allows for brush replacement then replace the brushes at the intervals recommended by the manufacturer. Those intervals are usually stated in hours of operation. If you have an RC aircraft with a brush type motor, it might be a good idea to keep a record of time used on the motor. This will help you know when to replace brushes.

Keep in mind that worn brushes will not only cause the motor to run poorly but will also reduce its efficiency and increase the sparking and noise that goes with the sparking. In other words, it's just not a good idea to fly with worn brushes.

Some brush type motors also have shaft bearings that need to be lubricated. If your motor requires lubrication of bearings use light weight machine oil and use it very sparingly. Wipe off excess oil as it will attract and catch dirt and dust and form a sludge type substance on the

Brush type motors should also be cleaned on a regular basis as well. Brush wearing with product carbon dust and the air vents on the motor will allow dust and dirt to enter the motor. You might wish to blow out the dust and dirt with a LOW VOLUME compressed air of even by just blowing in it if compressed air is not available. Again, follow the manufacturer's recommendations first if they have any.

Brushless motors really have no maintenance. There are no brushes to replace and other than keep the motor itself clean; there is little else to do. Most brushless motors have sealed bearing which means that not only do you not have to oil them, you shouldn't oil them. Just follow the manufacturer's instructions.

Care and Use of your Electric Motor

Electric motors are reliable and will take a lot of abuse. But there are a few things you need to be aware of to get the most out of your motor and also get the most life out of it as well.

Keep Propellers and Other Items Balanced!

One of the ways to ruin a good motor is to operate it with an unbalanced load. Having an unbalanced propeller or object attached to the shaft will create a lot of vibration. This vibration will cause abnormal wear on the shaft bearings and cause premature failure of the motor.

This vibration will get worse as speeds increase so if you should notice something wrong, and you cannot totally shut off the motor, lower the speed as much as you can in order to land the aircraft.

Use the Right Battery

Motors will quickly get destroyed if you connect a battery that has too high a voltage. It will burn out the motor and possible the motor and the controller. Only use batteries that are approved and rated for the type motor you are powering. Contrary to what some believe, using a higher voltage battery will NOT get you better or longer operation. It could actually give you worse operation or no operation at all. Ever.

Do Not Fly on a Discharged Battery

Discharged batteries have lower voltage and that can harm a motor. When a motors voltage gets too low sometimes the motor will try and draw more current and this can cause things to overheat and fail prematurely. Most motors and controller today have fail safe circuits to protect against this sort of thing but why take the chance if you don't have to. If you notice a battery getting low, land and replace it or recharge it.

Keep Motor Away From Extreme Temperatures

Nothing electronic likes things too hot or too cold.

Cold motors tend to use more power and that reduces flight time so try and keep things in the acceptable temperature rang. Your owners or operating manual will most probably give you the safe range of temperatures that you can safely fly. But remember, the lower the temperature the less the flight time.

Watch Motor Speed and Load

Motors have maximum speed and load limits. You should never operate your motor beyond those limits and it is a good idea to keep under those limits to protect the motor from excessive heat and stress. Just because something can go that fast doesn't mean it is smart to always push something to its limits!

How Many Channels Do You Need?

One of the most common questions people have when getting into RC aircraft is how many channels should they have on their new aircraft. Even those who have been in the hobby for a while are unsure what they need or should buy. For that reason we will discuss channels and how you should make your decision.

First of all, there is no right or wrong answer. Everyone is different and everyone is looking to get different things out of their RC flying experience. Some people just love to get their plane or copter in the air and fly it around in a circle and relax. Others want to do fancy maneuvers and tricks and that kind of stuff. Neither approach is right or wrong. Everyone should do what they enjoy and not worry about what the other person is doing. We are out to have fun and that's about it.

With that being said, there is a cost to all of this technology and we want to make the best decisions NOW so that we make the most out of our money and purchase.

The one thing we don't want to do is drop a few hundred on an aircraft now and find we have outgrown it a month later. So this is kind of a balance. Getting what you need not only for today but for next month or year as well.

The more complex your electronics are and the more you want to control the higher the cost is going to be. It just makes sense that a two channel system is going to cost far less than a 7 channel system. If it didn't, everyone would buy the 7 channel unit and just use the channels they needed at the time. But that would make things too easy and one thing manufacturers never seem to do is make things easy!

Most systems today start with 2 channels and work their way up to 7 channels and probably more. Each channel lets you control one part of the RC aircraft. The more channels you have the more control you have and the more you will be able to do with the airplane.

Two channel units are really considered toys as they really do not allow you to do too much other than take off, make rough turns and rough landings. You are really at the mercy of wind and other conditions when you try and take off or land a 2 channel plane. But 2 channel planes are the least expensive and many people start with them to see if they will enjoy flying.

While there is logic to that, you should be cautioned that a two channel plane sometimes will take away some of the enjoyment of flying. It is more difficult to take off and land a plane without elevator control which requires a 3 channel unit.

When you just have control over the propeller and tail rudder, flying is too basic. So you might get frustrated with a 2 channel unit and overall experience less enjoyment.

But if you are trying to introduce your child to RC flying, a 2 channel units might fit the bill nicely. They are inexpensive which means less is lost in a crash and they are easier to fly because you only have to worry about 2 things. But since kids usually pick this kind of stuff up faster than us adults, they might tire of their 2 channel unit even faster than we would!

For those reasons and a couple more, I suggest starting out with a 3 or 4 channel outfits. The third channel will add elevator control which helps you take off and land easier and also helps you climb and descend more accurately as well. If you go with the 4 channel unit you will add control over the ailerons which are wing surfaces that also help you turn and maneuver the aircraft.

The more channels you have the more difficult flying your plane will be but you will also have more control as well. You will be able to guide the plane more accurately and make tighter turns, more daring climbs and descents and also do maneuvers like barrel rolls and other tricks. But as we said, flying will be more difficult until you get the hang of it.

Once you go above 4 channels you get into things like controlling landing gear, lights, cameras and other options that the larger and more complicated aircraft might have. This is usually reserved for experienced pilots and very few beginners or novices will have, or even should have, those types of aircraft.

The key to channels is to have enough to do what you want to now and also have some flexibility and room to grow into. Having a 3 channel or 4 channel plane will give you enough control and flexibility to keep you engaged and happy for some time. If you can afford one of those models that should be the best way to go.

Once you get above 4 channels the cost can go way up and complexity increases and features increase. So as we said before, this is always going to be a balance between the features you want and the cost involved in getting the equipment.

If I were to sum things up in one paragraph, I would say to get a 3 or 4 channel unit with an emphasis on quality. You will have that and enjoy it for a very long time. If you buy a cheap 2 channel aircraft the quality isn't going to be there and you might get disappointed and turned off by the experience.

Consult your local hobby store about the models they have that fit your needs. You might be able to buy an expandable unit that will let you fly with 3 channels now and expand to 4 or 5 later on as your skills grow and you become more comfortable flying your aircraft.

Control Systems

In order to fly an RC aircraft, we have to have a way for recreating the actions of our hands on the controller to corresponding movements in the aircraft as it flies. The system used to accomplish task is called the control system.

An RC control system involves 3 basic parts. They are the transmitter, receiver, and on board controllers/servos. Each one of these parts has its own specific function. Here is what each part of the control system does:

Transmitter

The transmitter is the handheld device which you use to control how the aircraft flies. It holds the controls and the electronic transmitter that turns your hand movements into electronic signals.

The stronger the transmitter the larger the flight area can be. The more powerful the signal leaving the antenna the further away the plane can fly while still remaining in contact with the pilot.

Transmitters are usually sold in pairs with their corresponding receiver. If specific frequencies are needed then both the transmitter and receiver will be set for the same frequency. This allows other aircraft using different frequencies to fly in the same air space with conflicting with each other.

Transmitters will either work on the FM band of frequencies usually in the 27MHZ to 72MHZ if you buy an older system. Most of the newer systems are digital systems operating in the 2.4GHZ band. More on that later.

Receiver

The receiver is the part of the electronic control system that receives the signal from the transmitter and converts it into the individual channel signals which are sent to the other controls. The receiver is mounted somewhere in the aircraft and is powered by either the main battery along with the main motor or has its own separate battery just for the control system.

The receiver is important because the ability to accurately capture a signal and process it correctly is the heart of any control system. The transmitter and receiver are not areas where you want to skimp and get the cheapest. Instead, you should invest in a quality receiver / transmitter system that will give you good range and clear signals.

As we have said before the receiver must be matched with the transmitter and be able to recognize signals from that particular receiver and send them to the onboard control systems.

Part of the receiver includes the antenna which is either built into the structure of the aircraft or is a piece of wire strung on or over the aircraft body. The antenna receives the signals and sends them to the receiver for processing.

Controllers / Servo System

So far we have created the signal by physical movements of the controls and then taken those signals and sent them up to the aircraft. We then had the receiver "decode" those signals and break them down into the different channels. Now we have to take those individual signals and turn them back into physical movements within the aircraft which enable us to control the flight.

The devices that turn the electronic signals into physical movements are called **servos** or **controllers** depending on the application. A servo is a device that accepts an electronic signal and turns a wheel or lever in direct proportion to that signal.

A controller is a device that takes a signal and turns it into a varying voltage. For example, the main motor which turns the propeller is driven by an electronic speed controller or ESC. This device takes the signal from the receiver and either increases the motor speed to climb or go faster or reduces the motor speed to slow down or descend. While there is no physical movement taking place, the signal is converted into a particular voltage based on the signal coming in.

For the most part servo movements are linear which means they follow the direction and amount of movement the joystick makes. So moving the joystick to the right will make the servo arm or lever turn to the right as well. Move the joystick a little and the servo moves a little. Move the joystick a lot and the servo moves a lot. This enables us to make both small and large movements. Servos are not on/off devices like switches, they are more like variable controls that have infinite degrees of adjustment.

Motor controllers are usually linear as well although some can be programmed to behave in different ways based on the function and the motor being controlled. You don't need to understand all of this. You just should understand so you know what should happen should you have to troubleshoot a problem.

Naturally there will be a servos or controller for each channel. So a 6 channel aircraft would have 6 servos and or controllers, one for each function. Servos and controllers are connected to the receiver by a wiring harness which usually has sockets on the receiver that the servos or controllers plug into. In some cases where everything is not purchased together there could be hardwired connections secured by screws or other methods.

What Type of System? FM or Digital???

There are different systems available when it comes to controlling our aircraft.

There are the older systems which use transmitter tuned to the 27MHZ – 72MHZ FM band.

Transmitters and receivers operating on this band need to have their own independent frequency and no one else in the area can operate on the same frequency.

When you are flying with a club or group of people this is usually not a problem as everyone will know what everyone else is flying on. Each transmitter will be assigned a different frequency and there are usually colored flags that are attached to the transmitter antennas to let other people know what frequency you are flying on.

The problem is that a lot of people are not considerate and care only about themselves. So they arrive and do not bother to check what anyone else is doing and they just unpack and power up and send their plane off in the sir. Then they transmit on someone else's frequency and both aircraft get confused and nothing good happens. The result is one person yelling at another and no one goes home having a good day.

Fortunately, there are newer systems that use digital controls that eliminate this from happening. These systems transmit on a much higher frequency 2.4 GHZ which allows more range with less chance of interference as well. The transmitters and receivers are paired together and operate as one. They will not interfere with others using the same frequency range because each receiver was paired to just the one transmitter.

There are two different types of digital systems and both are equally good performers. The two types are DSSS (Direct Sequence Spread Spectrum) and FHSS (Frequency Hopping Spread Sequence.) As we said both of these systems perform well. Some manufacturers use just one of the systems while other manufacturers use the other.

The main difference between the two systems is that the DSSS use a constant small part of the frequency spectrum and the FHSS system hops around the entire spectrum according to the signals being sent. That's all you really need to know other than the digital systems perform better and eliminate the interference problem with other flyers.

Speaking of interference, it must be stated that the older systems operating on the FM band had a huge problem with electronic interference from motors and tools and other devices. The digital systems have almost eliminated this issue and are almost immune to interference and distortion of the signal.

Transmitter Care and Operation

Transmitters are very straightforward and easy to operate devices. They require no special instruction or knowledge to operate and there are few maintenance issues as well.

The main concern you should have with your transmitter is how you power it. While some transmitters do come with rechargeable batteries, others might state to use alkaline batteries which are not rechargeable.

Since the voltage of rechargeables is lower per battery, make sure your transmitter can work as designed with rechargeable batteries. Consult your owner's manual or contact the manufacturer for more information.

Since transmitter use moveable controls, it is important that you keep the transmitter clean and dust free after flight. If dust or dirt winds up on the surfaces of the controls this can lead to erratic operation and noisy signals. With today's receivers and transmitters becoming so fast and responsive, noisy controls could make the servos and controller system makes unwanted movements.

As far as receivers are concerned always make sure the battery powering the receiver has a good charge and do not just forget about it. On aircraft that use the same battery for propeller and receiver that is no issue. But when two individual batteries are used we sometimes forget about the control battery and just recharge the propeller battery. The result is a plane that now has a lot of power to fly wherever the heck it wants to because we can no longer control it!

Sound Systems

One of the "problems" associated with electric RC devices is the lack of sound that they make. While this might be appreciated by everyone else in the flying area, pilots who crave realism may not like a whisper quiet aircraft.

To resolve this issue some manufacturers have developed sound systems for their aircraft that mimic the sounds of real life plane in flight. So you can purchase an after-market sound system and get the real life sounds you expect when you see a plane flying high.

You should be aware that these systems do require power in order to function and that power sometimes comes from your on-board batteries. This means lower flight times. They also take up room and have weight so you should make sure your aircraft has the ability to add one of these systems on board if it did not come with one originally.

The sound systems can be programmed or purchased for specific model sounds and include sounds when idling, flying and landing. Some of the sounds are very realistic and the cost of these systems is not that expensive.

The casually flier might not be interested in these systems or see the value but an experienced flyer might just love hearing the sound of his or her plane cruising around above them. Like most other aspects of RC aircraft, it's all about fun and if hearing some familiar or nostalgic sounds makes everything more fun, who is to argue?

Flight Simulators

Sometimes even the smallest trainer aircraft can cost over $100-$200. While this is not a tremendous amount of money, it is still a sizeable investment for some people and not something you want to use once or twice and then throw away. Because of this many people are hesitant to take their aircraft out for the first time and fly it. This is because they are afraid of crashing and damaging their aircraft.

While RC flying is not difficult, many people prefer a less "dangerous" way of learning. Books like this help and give people a great understanding of how to fly and how to properly handle their aircraft, but nothing is better than putting the controller in your hands and actually flying. But along with that comes risk.

This is where flight simulators come into play. Flight simulators are computer programs that use your computer monitor as a learning tool.

These programs come with a controller that looks and feels like a real RC transmitter or they will use your existing transmitter is it is compatible and the program allows for that. Either way, instead of having your own aircraft in the air, you fly on your computer screen.

Flight simulators have realistic scenery and the view from your monitor will give you the feeling of flying. Each movement of the joystick will cause the appropriate movement of the aircraft just like in real life. The only difference is that when you do something wrong, the aircraft on the screen crashes not the one you bought that is sitting on your desk!

Flight simulators are good for two applications. The first is for entertainment when it is too cold or nasty to fly. Some pilots find using simulator programs to be a lot of fun. There are people who never fly a real aircraft but instead just love using the simulator. Either way is fine because all we are talking about is having fun, right?

The primary purpose of the simulator is to provide risk free practice. Practice so that instead of learning in the air and risking a crash, you learn inside and can make mistakes without risk. Flying is not intuitive at first and you might make the wrong moves unintentionally. If you are flying high enough you can recover. But if you make those mistakes taking off or landing, you could crash.

Using a simulation program lets you practice until you are doing things without thinking.

You can take off and land until it is second nature. If you crash, well you just start over. But hopefully you will have learned from your mistakes and next time things will be a little different.

Flight simulators also help people get into the hobby and stay with it. It is easy to get excited and purchase your first aircraft. But if you go out to fly it and come home with it in pieces, that is not fun. Some people get turned off so much by that experience that they just quit right there and look for something else. Taking the risk and bad experiences out of the equation at the beginning allows people to have more fun and get more involved and skilled.

As with most other products in life there are several different levels of flight simulators. You can get programs that mimic specific types of aircrafts and programs with more features and accuracy. As we stated before you can purchase simulators that come with their own controller or you can use your own. Naturally if you are new to the hobby and have not purchased your first aircraft yet, you won't have a controller. In those cases you would purchase a simulator with its own controller and start learning. As we said already, many people just enjoy flying with the simulator and never purchase a real plane. In those cases, you would just get a program with a controller included.

There are just a couple of things to be aware of when deciding which flight simulator to purchase.

The first is the type of computer you have. If you own a Windows based computer you should be fine as most of the simulator programs are designed to run on Windows because it is the most popular computer platform.

But if you own an Apple Mac, then you need to find a program that is compatible with that platform. Be aware that there are software applications that allow you to run Windows on a Mac so this might be an option as well.

The second thing is that flight simulators are available for both helicopters and airplanes. Unfortunately most are one or the other. There are a couple that support both so if you are looking to get into both helicopters and airplanes, then get a dual model version if available.

As we have said the primary difference between simulators is the graphics and accuracy. Any simulator will help you learn but the better ones are more realistic and enjoyable. After all you want to see what is really happening not some really poor graphical representation that you have to struggle to figure out.

Our suggestion is to stay away from the really cheap versions. They are cheap for a reason and it usually isn't because the manufacturer is a really nice guy. They are cheap because the quality is poor or standard features are lacking.

You don't have to get the top of the line either unless there are specific features that are really important to you. Instead, go for a mid range model that will give you high quality graphics and a good deal of realism. This will enable you to get the practice you need without risking your own aircraft.

No matter which model you purchase, let me leave you with one important message. Flight simulators of any kind are not 100% accurate. They do not take into consideration a sudden gust of wind or the occasional bird or other object flying into your flight path. These are designed to help you learn the controls in a straight forward and risk free manner. They are not designed for special or unique circumstances.

Flight simulators do not guarantee that you will not crash your first time out either. You will be nervous but probably a lot less nervous after you have taken off and landed 25 times without a crash on your computer. But you still will be nervous and you might make a mistake. Flight simulators will not protect you against that.

Last, but not least, flight simulators are only as good as the person using them. If you buy one and don't use it, it will not help you. But if you dedicate some time and practice flying on a simulator, you will most definitely have a much more rewarding and fun first time experience really flying your own plane outside.

RTF, ARF, or Kits?

As if this should be a shock to anyone, some pilots are actually builders and model enthusiasts at heart. Not only do they enjoy flying their airplanes and helicopters, they enjoy building them as well. Because these people have a wide range of skills, RC enthusiasts have a few options when it comes to how they purchase their aircraft. Those are RTF, ARF and kit form.

RTF stands for ready to fly and these units are almost totally assembled and wired for you. In some cases you just unpack, charge the batteries and off you go. For some of the larger models, you might have to attach the wing assembly and plug in the wing servo cable. That is because the wings are too large to attach to the plane and then put in a box. In any case, RTF is the choice for people who don't want to waste any time getting into the air.

If you do not have any desire to build your new aircraft, or if you know you don't have the skills required to do so, RTF units are probably your best choice.

There is nothing for you to mess up and no frustration in trying to do something you don't enjoy or have the aptitude for.

Flying an RTF unit is no less rewarding because it is the exact same plane or helicopter. Unless building it carries a special significance to you, consider taking the safe and easy way out and purchase an RTF. This is a good choice for the beginner because an aircraft that is already built will be easier to fly. When you build your own aircraft there might be small corrections that need to be made after flight. That is because how we build the aircraft, how much glue is used, and the quality of the construction will all have an impact on how well the aircraft flies.

Cost wise RTF's will be the most expensive although this is not usually a determining factor. Most often the reason to purchase an RTF is time and personal preference and has little to do with cost. When you compare prices, some ARF models will be more expensive but the quality you wind up with is probably higher. RTF trainers and other low cost aircraft are usually cheaper than most ARF's.

The next choice you might have would be an **ARF** which stands for almost ready to fly. ARF models are partially built aircraft and you do the final assembly. You should plan on spending several hours assembling and ARF aircraft. Generally the wings and fuselage (body) are all assembled which saves you the lion's share of the work.

But you still have to mount the motor and electronics install the linkages and glue some of the sub assemblies together on the body.

This might seem easy but it does take some time and skill to do all of this and do it right. While it is not difficult, it is not a 45 minute process either. As we said, it takes several hours, maybe two weekends, in order to complete the aircraft. This is mostly because you have to glue surfaces and pieces together and this requires time for the glue to set and harden before you can go on to the next step. You will not be working two weekends straight but rather short period of time followed by waiting for the glue to harden.

ARF's require tools to complete and these are usually miniature tools that the average person might not have. It should be worth noting that you will eventually need these tools for maintenance and repairs to your RTF aircraft anyway so purchasing them is still something you would have to do if you remain in the hobby for a while. There is also a process for adjusting and testing the aircraft after you complete it. This includes balancing the aircraft and doing test flights to fine tune everything.

ARF aircraft sometimes come in two forms. One is just the aircraft itself and does not include the motors or electronics and control systems. Those need to be purchase separately. The other option is to purchase a complete kit that includes everything. The complete kit is usually your best option.

When you purchase parts separately you have to make 100% sure that they are compatible with your particular aircraft. Just because they fit does not mean they will work. You need to be concerned with weight and servo movement and linkages and everything else. There is usually a lot of trimming and cutting and customizing required when you purchase things separately.

When you purchase everything in one box you are assured that everything will fit and the final aircraft will be properly balanced and set up for flight. Unless you have a ton of experience and patience, go with a complete kit. If you must purchase things separately, go to a reputable hobby or RC store and have someone there put together a package for you based on your personal needs and specifications.

As far as whether an ARF is right for you, I would say a few things. First, you need to have the skills and abilities to accomplish the building process. Second, you need the time and the space. You will have to have space for parts to sit undisturbed in order to dry during assembly. Third, and this is probably the most important, you need to enjoy doing this kind of thing. If you are not going to enjoy the process, there is little reason to go through it. This should be all about increasing your fun and enjoyment and not decreasing it.

Because of all of the above purchasing an ARF unit should not be about the money.

If you are not going to enjoy the process or possess the skills required to wind up with a quality product, you should stick to an RTF unit and just have fun with it.

Last, but not least, you can opt for buying your airplane or helicopter in kit form. I should state right now that this is definitely NOT an option for first time fliers or for people without some serious skills and a LOT of time to dedicate to the process.

Building any aircraft from scratch is a difficult and painstaking process. Not only do you have to concern yourself with a good looking final product, it also needs to be built almost perfectly in order for it to fly correctly and easily. Even something as small as using the right amount of glue on all surfaces can affect the way the aircraft performs.

The time required to build an aircraft of any type from a kit is a LOT of hours. You need to have some serious skills when it comes to cutting, trimming attaching the cloth or plastic covering and working with wood, metal and plastics.

While I am not trying to scare anyone away from kits, I just want to say that you should do a real honest assessment of your skills and abilities prior to making your kit purchase. This is definitely not something for a beginner or novice and you should have at least some background on flying and model building before you even consider building from a kit.

Tools Required For ARF and Kit Building

If you decide on an ARF or kit aircraft, here is a list of the tools and supplies you are likely to need. This should not be considered a full or comprehensive list as every model or kit will have different requirements. But this list will be a good start.

Small jewelers screw drivers
Small wrench set
Small pliers, needle nose and curved end
Diagonal cutting pliers for cutting wires
Scissors
Tweezers
Hobby knife set
Small clamps
Hobby vise
Small soldering iron and solder
Toothpicks for spreading and removing excess glue
Rubber bands for holding glued parts together
Sandpaper
Files
Epoxy Cement and Plastic model cement
Work light
Small flashlight
Inspection mirror for seeing inside of body
Work mat for construction surface to protect table tops from glue and tools

This will give you a pretty good head start when it comes to setting up for working on your kit or ARF aircraft.

Your instruction manual should give you a list of tools and supplies you will need.

Before you Start

If there is one rule I would urge you to follow it would be to follow every instruction exactly how it is written and in the order that it is written. Do not skip around as some steps need to be completed before parts are glued. Once they are glued you might not be able to do some of the previous tasks. So keep everything in order and follow the manual exactly.

Second, and this is also extremely important, use the EXACT type of glue they specify for each assembly. Glues are chosen for a reason and different glues have different strengths and flexibilities. If you substitute wood glue for Epoxy on the wings for example, your flight time will be really short.

Dedicate an area where you can work and leave parts out. Choose an area out of the reach of curious children or daily activities. Also choose an area where the wife will not mind if stuff is left out to dry. Also keep in mind that comes of the glues and adhesives and paints have a smell to them and this might be objectionable to others. So choose a well ventilated area not only for the smells but for your health as well.

Don't rush things and do not cut corners. Take your time and you will be rewarded with a much better final aircraft.

Micro Aircraft

If anyone ever doubted that technology changes the way products are made, they need look no further than micro RC aircraft. These aircraft are so small that micro copters fit in the palm of your hand and micro plane are just a little bit bigger.

New manufacturing capabilities, new foams and plastics and the latest miniaturized electronics all combine to make an aircraft that was impossible a decade or so ago. Though some of these micro units are little more than toys, some of them are almost full functioning aircraft. The only thing missing on the helicopters is usually a tail rotor and wing ailerons on the airplanes.

The functionality of these aircraft will enable them to do most every normal flight maneuver but you probably will not be able to do stunt flying that requires tail rotors or wing ailerons. Some of the airplanes may have to be hand launched as well but will have landing gear in order to land.

But other than that, these are fully functional aircraft. Be sure to check out different models to get the one with the features you want such as the ability to taxi and take off if you want to do that. Some people do, some don't. It's a personal choice.

There are a few things you should be aware of when it comes to these micro aircraft. These concern their flight characteristics and other things that are important to know before you buy and before you fly. Here a few things you should know:

Flying Space

Micro aircraft do not take a lot of room to fly. In fact, these are the only planes that can really be flown successfully indoors! Now, by indoors we do not mean your living room or den. But you can easily fly them in a gymnasium or other indoor venue such as barns and warehouses. If you have access to one of these types of indoor facilities you have just turned RC flying into a year round hobby no matter where you live!

Keep in mind that these aircraft are small so you cannot fly them very far or very high. Otherwise you will lose sight of them quickly and nothing good ever happens from that! The range on the electronics is usually smaller anyway so that will limit your flying area and help you remain in visual contact.

Control Systems

Because micro aircraft can be flown indoors they sometimes come with infra-red control systems instead of the standard radio controlled systems. While this is perfectly fine for indoor flying, infra-red does NOT work very well outside and sometimes not at all in bright sunlight.

If you intend to fly only inside then infra-red should be OK. But if there is a possibility that you might wish to fly outside, find a radio controlled model to eliminate the sunlight problem.

Otherwise the control systems are similar to those on larger airplanes. A transmitter sends you control movements to a receiver which decodes them and sends them to the different areas of the aircraft.

Wind

Because these aircraft are so small and the motors so small, they also have to be very light in order to fly. This makes them easy to fly but also makes them very susceptible to winds and other air movement.

This does not make them very good candidates for flying on windy or even breezy days. If you want to fly a micro outside, and your control system allows you to do that, you need to pick almost an absolutely wind free day. That means if the flags are moving and the trees are swaying, your micro should stay inside.

Even flying indoors can be tricky if there are large fans or air movement from air conditioning or heating ducts. That air movement can and likely will affect the flight of the aircraft. So wherever you fly, make sure there are no wind currents that can pick up and take away your micro.

Damage

Because micros are so small, the size of the supports in the body and on the wings cannot be very thick or strong. This means the micro aircraft will not be as strong or sturdy as a full size aircraft.

But that is not that big of an issue because with the low weight of the aircraft there is little momentum generated by these micros in flight. Plus the extremely low weight provides a light impact on the structure when crashes do occur. All I all micros take a ton of abuse for their weight and size and just keep going.

Micro helicopters for example, can be crashed from a few feet over and over without serious damage. They can fly into walls and furniture and just suffer a few nicks on their rotor blades.

Care

Regardless of the size of your aircraft, it still requires care and a little TLC. Keep it clean and keep it functioning properly.

If you have small enough tools, make sure everything remains tight and well functioning. Just because it is small does not mean it's a toy. These are real RC aircraft and you should treat them as such.

Where & What to Buy???

There are zillions of electric RC aircraft out there and sometimes it's difficult to know which one is the right one for you. Even more confusing sometimes is where you should purchase you aircraft. Plus there is one thing most people don't even think about that could have a huge impact on your choice.

Buy the Right Type and a Name Brand Whenever Possible

First of all, most people purchase their RC aircraft because they like the way it looks. While there is nothing wrong with that, you should always keep your current skill level in mind when deciding what to purchase. It is all right to buy something just a little past your skill level because you can grow into it. But a beginner should not be purchasing a $2,000 RC airplane to learn on.

Name brand units are a good choice because companies do not stay in business for long periods of time if they build and sell crap.

Do your research and look at a lot of different choices. Talk to local hobby store owners and even a few fliers if you know any. This is all part of the fun and you shouldn't pass over this exercise. After all the best decisions are informed decisions.

As to where you should buy your RC aircraft, you should factor in a few different things.

Should You Buy Locally or Over the Internet?

Buying locally will enable you to get more help and support when you need it. The hobby store can also assist you in getting replacement parts and other things when the need arises. You cannot always get that from a website 14 states away.

That being said, large online retailers such as Amazon are well known for their customer support and they stand behind everything they sell. Check the price of several different sources. If the online price is similar to the local price, then buy it locally. But if the model you like is a lot cheaper at an established and well known online site then buy it there.

If you are purchasing online I strongly urge you to see what you are purchasing at a local shop first. It is difficult to get an accurate idea of size and appearance from a little, or even big, picture. What looks great on a webpage can look like a colossal piece of crap when you open the box.

Crash Warranties or Insurance

Some companies offer crash insurance on some of their units. This might be worthwhile if you are just learning. If you do decide to purchase one of these policies make sure you understand what is covered and how you get your plane repaired.

Does it cover just parts or parts and labor? Who pays for shipping? Can it be fixed locally? What is the approximate turn-around time? What happens if the plane is damaged beyond repair? What happens if parts are no longer available? These are all questions you should have answered before you commit to purchase.

Spare Parts

This is one area where many people do not even think about when purchasing their new aircraft. If you purchase an aircraft that you cannot buy parts for, you might find yourself with a useless aircraft when you break a 25 cent part. Always make sure you know where and how to get replacement parts.

The best solution is to buy a make and model that is sold and supported locally. So whenever you need a part you can walk into the store and either order it or get it. This is one of the advantages of buying locally. Since you bought the aircraft from the store they have a vested interest in keeping you happy so you will buy your next one from them.

Wing Configuration

When it comes to RC airplanes, the configuration of the wings has a definite effect on the way the plane handles and flies. This is important for beginners especially because it should be a factor to consider when purchasing your first RC aircraft.

Wings and the way they are mounted have a direct effect on the stability of the aircraft and its ability to fly consistently without constant input from the pilot. Wings mounted on the top of the aircraft are more stable in flight than wings mounted lower or on the bottom of the aircraft. That is why you see the majority of trainer aircraft with their wings mounted high.

These are called **high wing** models for obvious reasons. The high wing models will be easier to fly but will still be able to do all the maneuvers you desire and provide full functionality. High wing models are more stable and they also make it easier to recover from mistakes or pilot errors.

The other factor when considering your first aircraft, or if you are still a beginner of sorts is the size of the wing. Generally speaking the larger the wing span the more lift those wings will provide. But that does not mean you can go larger and larger without sacrificing agility and performance.

Beginner and novices should look for an aircraft with a wing span of approx 30-50 inches. This will give you the wing size you need for stability while also giving you the lift you need. In addition, the aircraft will still be responsive and not so large and bulky that it flies sluggishly and requires a lot of room to fly.

If you are a more advanced flier and intend on doing a lot of performance or stunt flying, then a lower winged aircraft might be better suited to your needs. Mid wing aircraft are also suitable for stunt flying and also have high agility and response.

Today's model RC airplanes are all a lot more stable than they were in the beginning. Changes in materials have made these planes lighter and easier to fly. These changes make every plane today a lot easier to fly than the first RC planes. But if you are a real beginner or novice, then a high wing plane will be even easier.

Don't be afraid to try and fly any RC plane if you already own one or have access to one. Just be aware when you fly any aircraft that high wing aircraft will require less overall effort and input than the low winged aircraft.

But if you are into stunt flying and complex maneuvers, a low or mid wing plane might be the best choice.

Most of the time wing configuration is just a result of the type and model of aircraft. If you want something that looks like a World War 2 fighter airplane then you will have to go with a low wing design. But a pleasure aircraft could go either way and you could opt for a High Wing Cessna look alike for your choice.

Pre-Flight Procedures

When it comes to flying any type of aircraft, whether it be a helicopter, airplane, blimp or glider there are a few things that everyone should do to increase their enjoyment and protect the aircraft and those around it from injury. In this chapter we will discuss some of the checks and procedure every pilot should go through every time they fly.

Charge Batteries

Yeah, I know, this is common sense. But a lot of people think they have already charged the batteries and they drive an hour or so to a beautiful spot and nothing works because the batteries are dead. To avoid this I suggest always charging the batteries before each flight.

If you charge them after the flight then put a piece of tape with the charge date on the battery.

This not only reminds you that they were charged but also gives you an idea of when that charging took place. If it was yesterday or the day before that's fine. But if it was 4 months ago, you really should consider a re-charge. This holds especially true for NI-CAD batteries.

Check the Aircraft Before Leaving the House

There are checks that should be done to any aircraft every time before you fly. These checks include making sure everything on the aircraft looks all right and operates freely and as it should. If there are any problems such as broken parts or binding linkages, these should be repaired before flying the aircraft. While some pilots do this on the air field, I prefer to do this before I leave for a couple of really good reasons.

First, it is just easier to take care of repairs inside where you have a table or a bench with decent lighting. It just makes things easier to see and easier to work on. You probably have more tools at home than you take with you and this also makes repairs go easier and faster.

The first check you should do is a quick visual check to make sure the body is intact and that nothing tore through the exterior or caused any other type of damage. Aircraft skins and bodies can be fragile and it doesn't take much to damage them at times.

Even if damage doesn't look that bad it should be fixed before the next flight for two reasons.

First the damage could get worse in flight. Second, the damage might alter the flight characteristics of the aircraft and cause you real problems in the air. A rip in the exterior covering, for example, can cause air patterns to form and make the aircraft unstable. So just take care of the problems before flight and not worry about them anymore.

Linkages and mechanical checks should be next. There is a lot of vibration and buffeting that occurs in flight and this can make screws and bolts and nuts loosen up over time. You should make sure everything is tight and function well.

All control surfaces and linkages should operate smoothly and freely. If something is binding or operating roughly it will affect the flight of the aircraft. Check the operation of everything and correct any problems you might encounter. As we have already said it is a lot easier to correct problems on the ground than it is to correct them in the air.

Lubricate and do any maintenance that might be required as well. Do not keep flying something without checking it just because it worked fine last time out. Things have a habit of happening on their own and we just want to try and take care of as many of them as possible before they cause problems.

Check the Weather

If it is going to rain or if there is lightning in the forecast, stay home. It is not worth the risk to your equipment or your life to fly in dangerous weather.

The same goes for snow and sleet. Ice and snow can build up on the wings and body and the added weight can make the aircraft plummet to the ground.

If there is considerable wind in the area, consider not flying that day either. The smaller and lighter the aircraft the more it is going to be affected by the wind. The more a plane is moved by the wind the more skill it is going to take to keep it flying the way you want it to. Beginners and novices might not have those skills yet and should avoid windy or even breezy days until they get more practice.

Visibility can be an issue as well. Fog will keep you from keeping your aircraft in eye contact and you could lose the aircraft or fly into something because you couldn't see t. do not fly by listening to the motor. First of all electrics do not make much noise and bird don't make any when they are flying. So be a friend to the birds and to your aircraft and only fly when you can see where you are going.

Fog and visibility often change according to altitude. For example, you might be able to see for a mile on the ground but 100 ft up there is fog and you will lose sight of the aircraft. So be aware of all weather conditions before sending your aircraft up. Never fly during any conditions that make you lose sight of the aircraft and the area that it is flying into. There is just too much chance of harm to others and your aircraft.

Check Tools and Supplies

If you do not have a flight box to store all you accessories, supplies and tools you should invest in one. It doesn't have to be anything fancy or even something manufactured for RC flight equipment. Just a regular toolbox will fit the bill nicely.

You can keep spare parts like propellers and hardware in small plastic boxes or containers with dividers in them. This makes it easy to see what you need and to also let you know when you are running low on something.

Always check you box to make sure you have everything you need before you leave the house. If you forget your batteries, flight time will be shorter than expected. If you should forget a tool or two, you might not be able to make repairs on the field. Neither of these are good to happen.

When t comes to batteries, make sure they are fresh and not too old. Cycle through your batteries using the oldest first so that no battery just sits there until it is too old to use any more. Label your rechargeables with the date they were purchased so you will know which batteries are which when it comes time to decide which ones to use.

Before Take Off

You are never too careful when it comes to pre-flight checks. Before you actually take off, power up the aircraft and do one more final check of the movement of all the control surfaces.

Sometimes things happen in transport and what worked fine at home might not work so well right now.

Check the wind and the flight area for anything you need to be aware of such as too many people, wind gusts, storm clouds and anything else you can think of. One last confirmation for good visibility and you should be good to go.

The Golden Rule

While there are a number of things a pilot can do to keep his or her aircraft under control there is one very easy rule to follow that will not only make it easier and more enjoyable to fly, but will also greatly increase your level of fun and enjoyment as well.

Most of the problems and crashes that occur during RC aircraft flights are caused by human error. While this is not surprising in itself, the type of human error that is usually responsible, at least by beginners and novices, is easily preventable.

Most new or novice pilots do not realize that only small movements on controls are necessary for normal flight. In fact, not only are small and controlled movements all that are required, those are precisely the type of movements that always should be used.

Most crashes or problems occur when people make sudden and huge joystick movements.

Most of the time these are made when the pilot is scared and panics when something unexpected happens. They see a plane doing something they did not expect and their reaction is to make a huge and violent correction to stop the aircraft from doing what it is doing.

The most common reaction to a plane crashing is to either give it maximum power or to turn off power completely. While one of these moves might work, it is usually a soft and controlled reaction that will bring the best result. That means slowly raising the throttle or slowly reducing it and monitoring the reaction of the aircraft.

Another problem is using too much power too quickly and vice versa. If you go instantly from zero to full throttle the plane is not going to react in a controlled manner. It might suddenly pitch forward or veer to the side because of all the torque the body is experiencing from the drive motor. If the pilot steadily goes from zero to full throttle over the time of a few seconds, the aircraft will instead taxi and slowly rise into the air smoothly and under control.

The same goes for turns and other maneuvers. Giving an airplane full rudder in either direction will make for a sharp turn that just might thrown the aircraft into a spin or dive. But just a small movement of the rudder will cause a nice banking gentle turn that will be fun to watch by both pilot and spectators.

Flight should be smooth and graceful not violent and jerky. When we make small controlled movements, the result is that the aircraft flies in a very stable and controlled manner. That is what we are looking for. Every pilot should practice making smooth turns and smooth ascents and descents. This is how we improve our skills and abilities.

Whenever something unexpected happens, we need to respond in the same controlled and subdued manner. This might be difficult especially in the beginning when we are not all that familiar with how our planes or helicopters fly. When we are not familiar or confident, we tend to panic and panic usually does not mean small and controlled. Panicked means huge and uncontrolled.

We need to practice making small movements and seeing how the aircraft responds. Then we make other movements to see how the aircraft responds to those movements. By continuing to do this we gain an understanding on what has to be done in which circumstances.

For example, let's say your airplane catches a gust of wind and goes into a sharp right turn. The correct way of recovering from such a situation is not to take the controller and make a hard left turn. That would just cause the plane to either tailspin or otherwise go out of control. The correct way is to slowly bring the aircraft out of its turn and then make a slow left turn to get back on course.

The cardinal rule is to always make small movements and monitor the result. If the result is what you want, then fine. If it does what you want but not enough then increase the same movement. But if it makes things worse, or has the opposite effect, back off and try something else.

Some people might say that sometimes you do not have the time to make these small corrections and wait for the results. In some cases you might be right but a smart pilot knows they should always fly at least "2 mistakes high" which means you should fly high enough so that you will have sufficient height and time to recover from two situations.

That is why flying low is actually more risky than flying high. If you make a mistake close to the ground, the plane might crash before you can react. In any case whether the aircraft is 2 feet or 200 feet off the ground you should only use small and controlled joystick movements to fly it.

This will become easier as you practice and practice. Eventually you will do things without thinking and all your movements will be small and controlled. This is when you realize that you are no longer a new or novice pilot. When you can respond to situations with controlled movements and without thinking about what you're doing, you have graduated to an experienced pilot.

All that being said, the only time you should make large or rapid movements will be after you become experienced and graduate into stunt flying. But for most of us that is a long way off and many of us will never get to that point and don't really want to.

So for now, let's just say always slow and always in control. That is the best way to fly an RC aircraft.

Flying Etiquette

Flying an RC aircraft should be a fun and enjoyable process. But that can only be when we behave and act in the proper manner. If everyone would follow a few simple rules the hobby would be much better off for pilots and spectators as well as the people living and using the areas in which we fly.

In order to make RC flying enjoyable for everyone, here are some easy to follow guidelines designed to protect both pilot and spectator:

Be Considerate of Others

The world does not revolve around you and your RC aircraft. Be considerate when it comes to the lives of others and how your flying in that area or at that time might affect others. Try to minimize the impact of your RC flying on others.

That also means behaving properly and not yelling or curse when something doesn't work right or when you crash.

No one needs to listen to an adult swearing a blue streak because their RC aircraft is lying in 12 pieces.

While flying behave yourself and watch what others are doing as well so you do not interfere with them.

Fly Only in Approved Areas

Do not fly where RC aircraft are not allowed to fly. Some public parks, private properties and other areas do not allow RC flying or trespassing of any kind. If in doubt, ask!

Do Not Fly in Crowded Areas

A lot of people, especially children do not mix well with RC flying. Natural curiosity will draw people towards you and your aircraft. Since rotating blades and propellers can cut and cause injury, crowds and RC aircraft are not a good mix. Compound that with issues involving crashes and injuries and it is just best to go where there are not a lot of people,

Keep Noise Down in Residential Areas

While electric aircraft do not make anywhere near the noise of the older gas models, they still make noise and you and your children will make noise as you fly as well. Don't fly early on weekend morning when things are very quiet and people are still sleeping.

Don't become a distraction at schoolyards or when others are having parties as well. Just be a good neighbor and consider others before deciding where and when to fly.

Watch Frequencies

Always know who is flying on which frequency. Not all transmitters can fly at the same time. Make it your responsibility to know who is flying where and under which frequency. Do not leave it to the other guy to do the checking!

Fly Safely

Keep fancy and stunt flying to remote areas where there are no other people around. Never use an RC aircraft to "buzz" or "dive bomb" others even if you know them and intend it to be a joke. It's not funny when someone gets cut by a propeller.

Do not take off in the direction of a group of people or land in a group of people either. Pick a relatively quiet area to take off and land.

Watch out for Children & Pets

Children and pets will naturally be attracted to you and your aircraft. Their natural curiosity can pose a problem for you whenever you fly. Children and animals might not know any better but you should. It is your responsibility to keep others safe when you are flying.

Right of Way

Unless you are flying on your own land, spectators and others have the right of way. You and your plane do not. The only exception would be a park or designated club flight field where RC flying is the primary purpose.

That means bike riders and picnickers and walkers have the right to spend their day without being affected by your aircraft. Again, just be a good neighbor.

Flight Clearance

Aircraft should never fly too close to one another. Maintain a safe and reasonable distance both in area and in altitude from other aircraft. Be aware of when others are taking off or landing and make sure to stay clear of all other aircraft while your aircraft is airborne.

Clean Up After Yourself

The parks are not a place for you to leave old batteries, lunch wrapper and damaged aircraft parts strewn all over. Make sure you leave the place as clean, if not cleaner, than it was when you got there. That is not only being a good neighbor, it is also being a good citizen.

Be an RC Ambassador

People will undoubtedly come up to you and ask you about your aircraft. Be nice to people and talk to them.

Tell them what a great hobby it is and show them how things work. You could make a new friend or get a new member for your club. Sometimes people need just a little bit of encouragement to get started and they will be grateful to you for providing it.

Cleared for Take Off!

Now is the time when we are just about ready to watch the propeller start spinning and watching our plane roll down the runway! This is a very exciting and rewarding time and you should enjoy it!

To make your take-offs go easier and have the best results, here a few tips and suggestions:

Nice Slow & Controlled Motions

We are going to repeat this same thing a few times throughout this book because it is one of the single most important aspects of RC flying. Whether you are flying an airplane or helicopter or even driving a remote control boat or car, everything should be done using small and smooth movements.

Do not jerk the controls rapidly to one side or another.

This will cause very large movements in the aircraft and can cause instability and loss of control. Small and smooth movements allow you to remain in control and able to make minor adjustments to have the aircraft do what you want when you want. This is the same for speed, turns, altitude adjustments and anything else. Smooth and controlled beats rapid and extreme every time.

This is important because when you get scared or afraid your natural tendency is to make huge corrections and not small adjustments. You need to practice controlling things with small movements so this becomes second nature to you. This way when something unexpected happens you will not panic and turn off the engine or bank the plane over on its side. You will just regain control and keep on flying.

Hand Launching

Some very small planes will not have landing gear which means they cannot roll down the runway. In other cases you might not have a surface where your plane can roll so a hand launch might be the only way to get your plane in the air.

To hand launch a plane, you hold it in one hand and use the other hand to hold the controller and bring the propeller up to about ¾ speed to max speed. Then you would push firmly forward and release the plane in a controlled and level manner.

Do not throw the plane upwards as this might cause a stall and a crash. Do not release it downwards either as this might cause it to just hit the ground! Release it level and firmly to give it enough initial speed that it will remain airborne.

Immediately after releasing the aircraft take the controller in both hands and start flying the aircraft using the same techniques and procedures listed below. Your first thoughts should be on making sure the aircraft has enough power to rise first. After you have confirmed that you can start your controlled ascent.

As with every flight maneuver and control, use small and controlled movements after hand launching.

The Runway

If your plane has landing gear, which most RC units do, then you would use a runway to launch your plane. The runway should be a smooth and fairly hard surface. Concrete or blacktop is great as long as it is smooth and without cracks or holes that could catch the landing gear wheels. While smooth and packed dirt can also be used, sand and soft dirt will make it almost impossible for the plane to roll along and take off.

Naturally the surface should be fairly level so the plane will not veer to one side during takeoff. The runway should be at least one and a half times longer than the amount of space needed to take off.

This will give you some extra room in case of issues with wind or speed or even to abort take off. Since you probably will use the same area for landing, it should be long enough to land the plane as well.

Fly Into the Wind!

You will have the best results when you take off into the wind. Having the wind against you will bring more air over the wing and improve the lifting ability of the wind. This will get you into the air faster and easier

Avoid trying to take off with a crosswind. This can make take off very difficult and might even cause the plane to roll to one side and crash right after take-off. This is because the plane is not going very fast and is more susceptible to cross winds on the ground than in the air.

Slowly Increase Power

Start the engine and gradually apply more power. It should take 2 or 3 seconds to go from zero to ¾ or full power. This will enable the aircraft to move forward in a controlled manner and not pitch forward or rise too quickly.

Another reason is something called "torque effect". This means that the aircraft might have the tendency to move to one side due to the force of the propeller turning too fast too quickly. This might make the aircraft roll over to one side and crash right after takeoff.

Keep the Plane Straight

The plane should go down the runway in a straight line. Use the rudder to control the plane and keep it straight. Sometimes the wind might cause the plane to move and small adjustments to the rudder will help keep it on course. Again, small correction movements are all that is required. Move the rudder too much and you will make the plane turn and roll off the runway or crash.

Use Elevator to Raise Plane

When you have built up some speed, use the elevator to gently raise the plane off the ground. Again, use small amounts of elevator to make a smooth and gentle ascent. If you use too much elevator you could make the plane rise too quickly and stall. If the plane stalls too close to the ground you might wind up walking over to pick up your aircraft in pieces!

Continue a Smooth Climb

After you take off continue a smooth climb until you reach the altitude you are comfortable flying at. You should always be high enough where you can recover from any problems but low enough to have the aircraft remain visible at all times.
Some beginner pilots are afraid to fly very high thinking that they are going to crash. So they stay lower in hopes of causing less damage.

In reality though, flying higher gives you a chance to recover from a control mistake before the plane hits the ground. You just make your correction and bring the plane back up to altitude.

When you fly too low and problems do not give you enough time to correct before the plane hits the ground. So do not be afraid to get the plane up to an altitude that is "one or two mistakes high".

As with anything you try for the first time, you might not do it perfectly. Some first time pilots like to practice" touch and lands" if they have enough room. This means they do a take off until the plane gets about a foot off the ground and then they bring it back down. They feel this allows them to practice take offs and landings without doing too much damage to the aircraft during the learning phase.

Keep in mind that your runway needs to be long enough to both take off and land at the same time. You will not be able to turn around at such low altitudes.

The main purpose here is just to get used to your aircraft and have a lot of fun! So practice makes perfect!

Helicopters

Helicopters do not exactly take off they lift off. There is no runway or taxiing involved. You just increase power to the rotors until the plane lifts off the ground. But like anything else, there are some things you should take into consideration when taking off.

First, make sure you advance the power slowly. If you go right to full throttle the helicopter will tend to rotate and you might lose control and crash before you know it. Slowly advance the power until you notice the helicopter is light on the skids. Advance it slightly more and you will rise in the air. If you have a tail rotor, adjust that to keep the helicopter stable and not rotating. Continue to rise and stabilize until you get where you want to be.

The one major difference between helicopters and airplanes is that a helicopter can safely fly just off the ground to minimize damage. Falling from 6 inches on a helicopter will not cause much damage but a 20 ft drop might.

Practice just barely lifting off and keeping the helicopter under control at low levels. When you can lift off and hover and then easily land you are ready to move on.

As with planes, small movements and doing things slowly is the key to the best take off. Once any RC aircraft loses stability it can be a real handful to recover. So keep everything under control and you should do just fine.

Flying Your RC Aircraft!

Flying your RC aircraft can be one of the most relaxing and enjoyable activities you can have when it comes to a hobby. There is just something special about watching something under your control flying around in the sky just like a bird.

Flying isn't difficult but you do need to know a few things to get you started. After a while experience will take you to the point when you can just fly without really concentrating on everything you are doing.

Here are some suggestions on how to get the best experience out of flying your aircraft:

Know Flight Time

Make a note of what time you took off you will know when you will have to land the plane so that fuel or battery power does not run out. Give yourself a buffer to compensate for reduced battery life and missed landing approaches. Some pilots like to have a 10% buffer. For inexperienced pilots, make that 20 percent.

Another factor that can significantly affect flight time and battery time is temperature. The colder the temperature the less time the battery will last. Wind and the amount of controlling the pilot has to make during the flight will also affect flight time. Exactly how much you won't know until you try but it will lessen the flight time. Just something to be aware of.

That means if you get 20 minutes of flight time on a charge or on fuel, your actual flight time should be approx 16 minutes from take off to landing. It is better to land a little early than to lose power a little late!

Know Your Flight Area

Have a picture of where you want to fly so that you will be able to anticipate when you will need to turn or make other maneuvers. Ideally you should do this before you take off but you can do it once you are in the air as well. Make sure the area you wish to fly in is well within your transmitters and receivers range. Always give yourself a buffer when it comes to range.

Keep in mind that buildings and large trees can interfere with RC flight in many ways. Try and map out your flight area so you can avoid these areas and have an obstacle free flight plan. Large building and metal structures may also block electronic signals and you definitely want to avoid that at all costs.

Reduce Power & Level Out

When you get up to the altitude where you want to fly, slowly (yes slowly) reduce power until the plane maintains altitude. If you reduce it too much the plane will start to descend. If that happens, just increase power to get the plane back up and then reduce it a little less to keep it at that altitude. Keep in mind that you will have to adjust power when you are flying with and against the wind. Again, make small corrections until this becomes second nature to you.

Always make sure you are flying at a high enough level that you will have time to make corrections for anything that might happen. 100-200 feet is a good altitude as long as you can see the aircraft in flight.

Practice Turns

Your flight time will be pretty short if you don't turn! So, use the rudder to gently turn the aircraft. Make small corrections at first until you get the feel for how your aircraft will respond. Accelerate slightly into the turn to keep altitude and then slowly use the rudder to bring the plane smoothly out of the turn and bring power down to where it was before the turn.

Some 4 channel systems will also provide you with control over the ailerons which are control surfaces on the wings themselves. These will help you turn and bank along with the rudder.

Some controller will actually let you control both with one movement. Check your transmitter manual to see if your transmitter has this type of mode of operation.

One thing that will require a little bit of thinking is that turns with the plane coming towards you will require movement of the stick in one direction whereas the same turn with the plane moving away from you will require movement to the other direction. This might be confusing to you at first but will quickly become second nature to you.

Turns are very important and this is an activity where novices and beginners often have problems. Keep in mind that small movements on the controls are all that you need and making a nice and graceful wide turn is preferable to a tight and sloppy turn that cause a crash! We are in this for the enjoyment not to see who can make the tightest turn.

Keep at a Safe & Steady Height

One of the most challenging parts of flying is keep the aircraft at a consistent height. This is done through the use of the throttle or propeller speed. Winds will affect the altitude as well as maneuvers such as turning.

It also takes some practice to notice changes in altitude. Since the plane is small and up quite high, you might not notice it rising or falling at first. Then, all of a sudden, you realize it is really, really high or really low. Don't panic just increase power if it is too low or reduce power if it is too high.

Again, use small movements and corrections and see how the aircraft responds. There is no need for massive changes in power or speed. Just nice gradual changes until you get the result you are looking for.

What is the Perfect Height?

There is no perfect height as most of it has to do with personal preference and the reason for the flight. If you are into fancy maneuvers and dives you might want to start higher. But for the average flier and especially the beginner, the perfect height should address two factors. Those are safety and visibility.

You should never fly an aircraft so high that you cannot see it or see what it is doing. This does not mean that you are going to see the rudder move or anything like that. But you should be able to watch it turn and notice significant changes in altitude. This height will depend on the conditions at flight time as well and the size and color of the airplane. Another factor is the eyesight of the pilot. So if you need glasses to see for distance, make sure you wear them.

The other factor is the issue of safety. You should always fly high enough so that you will have time to correct any errors or mistakes you made while flying. If you should make a drastic movement by mistake and cause the plane to dive, you should be at a height that gives you enough time to recover and make the right corrective movements.

This not only protects your aircraft but also anyone who happens to be on the ground near where the plane is flying.

Keep Aircraft In Front of You!

Never fly the aircraft over your head. This can get you disoriented and you might make the wrong choice of movements. Always keep the aircraft in front of you. You can manage this by turning as you fly so that you are always facing the aircraft. Never fly so far that you cannot see the aircraft. Never position yourself so the aircraft is behind you and you cannot see it.

Practice Flying in a Circuit

The first few times you fly you should concentrate on getting the plane up in the air and back down safely. But you are also going to need to learn how to fly and make turns as well. So why not combine the two and practice everything at the same time?

I suggest you plan out an area in the shape of a rectangle in the sky and take off and fly within that rectangle. You can use a visual marker to indicate the size of the rectangle or you can just picture it in your mind.

Take off and reach a comfortable altitude and then fly within that rectangle making turns whenever you reach a point near the corner of that imaginary rectangle. Accuracy is not as important as making nice smooth turns.

All your turns will be either right or left turns depending on the direction in which you are flying. Be aware though that stick movements moving towards you will be reversed from stick movements when the aircraft is moving away from you and vice versa.

Practice your turns until you can anticipate them and make then even and smooth. Use the rudder and throttle to make your turn and keep the same altitude. This will take practice so be patient.

Try and increase the power heading into the turn so you won't lose speed and altitude. Reduce the power coming out of the turn so you do not climb higher. Don't worry if your turns are early or late or if you gain or lose altitude. All of that will come from practice. For now just concentrate on doing this the right way. Use small and smooth movements and watch how the plane responds.

After you have flown a few circuits of your rectangle reverse the direction so you will practice making the other turns. If you had been making all left turns before, you will be making all right turns now. The movements are the same just the stick positions on the rudder will be different. Throttle, of course, remains the same.

As you get more comfortable making your turns and keeping your altitude steady, you might be ready to fly with more accuracy.

To practice this, pick some kind of marker in the sky, such as a cloud and practice turning at a specific point and exiting the turn at another specific point. This will help you fly more accurately and this will help you in making your landing approaches as well.

Trimming

Trimming your plane is the process by which you calibrate your transmitter and receiver to fly the plane straight ahead without any input or correction from you. If your transmitter has a trim function you will usually find those controls next to the joystick controls. They are usually slide type controls.

Fly the plane straight and take you hands off the controls, if the plane continues to fly straight, everything is fine. But if it veers to either side, move the trim control in one direction and straighten out the plane manually. Take your hand off the controls again. If it flies straight now, you're done. If it is better but still not right, move the trim control a little further. If it is worse, move the trim control in the opposite direction. Eventually you will find the "sweet spot" and your plane will fly straight.

If the plane should try and roll to one side, there are trim controls for that as well and they are adjusted in much the same manner. Move the control, test and readjust if necessary. Your transmitter manual will show you which controls are used for what function.

Why bother doing all of this if you can control it manually? Well, it is just easier and more fun to watch the plane in flight and not have to worry about constantly adjusting things to get it to fly straight. Since the primary objective is always to increase the level of enjoyment, it makes sense to have everything calibrated and working as well as possible.

Don't Fly Too Far

Always be aware of where your plane is in the sky at all times. Also know where the boundaries of your range are so you can keep your aircraft well within those ranges. Do not play too close to the end of the range because you might lose signal and control of the aircraft. Always give yourself some margin for error.

Also never forget that your range includes height as well! So if you are 200 feet up and your range is 1000 ft, you cannot fly 1,000 feet away because the height will add to the total distance. If you want to figure out approximate ranges you can use the following equation:

Range squared = height squared X distance squared.

This is just an airplane adaptation of the Pythagorean Theorem which most of us learned and then promptly forgot in Junior High School! Just remember to always factor in height when determining range and you will be just fine.

Don't Fly Too Low

As we already stated, flying too low reduces your time that you can recover from a problem and also creates a potential danger situation when it comes to spectators and others in the general area. Fly high enough to give yourself the time you need to make corrections and recover from mistakes. As you become more advanced and adept at the controls you can safely fly a little lower.

When Something Goes Wrong

When something goes wrong, and we say "when" because at some point or another something will go wrong, it is important that you remain calm and know what to do. After a while things will come so naturally for you that you won't even think about things like this. You will just do them automatically. But until then, here are a few suggestions to help you:

Stay Calm – It doesn't do you any good to panic. Panic makes you do things that you shouldn't do like go crazy and move controls all around thinking maybe you will get lucky and something will work. Trust me, it doesn't work that way. Stay calm and think about what you are doing.

Fly High – like we said, the higher you are the more time you have. Give yourself some peace of mind and security by flying high.

Use Small Movement – most flight mistakes can be easily resolved by making small corrective movements. If you make large movements you might overcorrect and cause another problem. Make a small adjustment and if that makes things better continue until things resolve themselves. If the small adjustments make things worse, then try something else.

Reduce or Cut Power – If nothing seems to work, try reducing speed or, in the case of an electric aircraft, stopping the engine all together. This will make it easier to control and might even cause the plane to start to glide. Then you can restart the motor, wipe the sweat from your forehead and put the grin back on your face! You can also use the elevator in glide mode as well as turn to correct the course.

There are two things you should be aware of when it comes to unexpected problems while in flight.

The first is that they are going to happen and you do have to deal with them. Sometimes you will be successful but other times, especially if there is an equipment malfunction or defect, you might not be able to do anything. You just have to take what happens and move on. It's part of the habit like striking out in baseball or throwing an interception in football.

The second thing is when something does happen and you are able to recover from it and keep the plane in the air that is a great feeling and your confidence shoots way, way high.

So don't be afraid and just do your best. After all, this isn't you life at risk, it's just a model plane. When you keep things in perspective it just makes life a lot easier!

The Perfect Landing!

What goes up must come down and RC aircraft are no exception! Once you take off, eventually you have to land. For some, landing is the most stressful and difficult part of the flight experience. That's because it is more difficult to land than it is to take off. But we can make it a lot easier if we just think it through.

Landing actually is a fairly simple and straightforward process that is easy to learn if you just take it slow and follow some simple steps. There are different procedures for landing both planes and helicopters.

When flying an RC airplane, here are the steps you should follow to have that perfect landing:

Land into the Wind

Landing into the wind allows the plane to travel slower and still remain airborne as it comes down. If you try to land with the wind the plane may "sail" and rise unexpectedly or be difficult to bring lower smoothly.

Give Yourself Plenty of Room

The rule of thumb for landing is that you should have roughly 150 feet of runway to land your plane. You don't really need that much but it is good to have if you land a little late or long on the runway. Having too much runway is not a problem. Running out of runway, though, can be a huge problem!

Take it Slow

Bring your plane down slowly. Have a controlled decent even if you have to make a few turns and fly around for a while to get to the right altitude to start your approach. Dropping too fast can cause your plane to become unstable and make it more difficult to control.

Your Approach

In order to have a good landing you need to think a few steps ahead. You need to position the aircraft in the air so it approached the runway in the right direction and at the right height. Too high and you will overshoot the runway and too low and you might land before the runway. Give yourself some room and take it slow and smooth.

You should approach the runway straight and centered on the landing strip. Do NOT try and turn your way onto the landing strip as you are landing!

Level & Straight

Keep the plane level and straight throughout your approach. Try and keep the aircraft centered on the runway to allow for any minor drift or movement.

Reduce Power Gradually

Reduce power gradually until the plane is just off the runway. Do not bring it down too fast or you risk damaging the landing gear.

Use Elevator to Bring Nose up Slightly

Use the elevator control to raise the nose slightly. And I mean slightly. Just a little bit is all you need. Too much and you will enter a stall and the plane will drop. This is called flaring the plane and will prepare it for touchdown.

Cut Power Completely

Cut off power to the main engine (propeller) if the approach is good and everything looks good. The plane will drop further and make contact with the runway. Some pilots like to cut the motor and glide in for the landing and this is perfectly fine if that is what you want to do.

Hit on Main Landing Gear First

You should touchdown using the main landing gear first followed by the nose gear.

The lighter the touch down the better the landing. But any landing that your plane survives without damage is a good landing! You don't have to be perfect you just have to get your plane back on solid land in one piece!

Missed Approaches

Sometimes things do not go as planned and you have to abandon that landing attempt. This happens to everyone and it is no big deal. When you find yourself in a situation where something isn't right, just increase power, take the plane back up and start your approach over again. This is one of the reasons why we want to have extra time and power available!

Missed approaches happen to everyone and it is nothing to be ashamed about. Wind gusts or air pockets can cause a plane to change position. Do not panic just take the plane back up and start over.

Once you have landing successfully, congratulate yourself on a job well done and consider the day and the flight a huge success! This is an important time because you have just proved to yourself that you can fly your plane and get it back to dry land safely. It is an important steps and it will give you confidence that will stay with you for a long time.

Landing a Helicopter

Landing a helicopter is not that difficult unless you try and land in the wind and then it can get dicey. The best thing to remember is that you want to reduce power gradually and bring everything in to a landing in a slow and controlled manner.

You should never try and land a helicopter, or any RC aircraft, in a crowded area. This presents a danger to everyone around. Even if you keep the aircraft away from people their natural curiosity might make them come to you causing problems and dangerous situations.

Leave Yourself Some Battery Power

When it comes time to land, first of all leave yourself a cushion of power so that you will be able to make a slow and controlled descent. Unlike an airplane, a helicopter cannot glide in for a landing. When the rotors stop it drops like a rock. So we want to make sure we get on the ground with some power left in the batteries.

Gradually Reduce Altitude

When you are ready to land slowly bring your helicopter down in a controlled manner. Do not abruptly shut off or drastically reduce power. This will make the copter fall and it might lose stability. Slowly bring it down stopping every now and then if the descent should become too fast.

Slow down the descent by adding a little bit of power. Bring it closer nice and slow keeping rotation to a minimum by using the tail rotor.

Slow When Close to the Ground

Slow your descent even more as you get closer to the ground. You want to come in very slow and gently touchdown. You don't want to bounce when you touch down as this might lead to the helicopter tipping over and damaging the rotor blades.

When you get to a foot to a few inches from the ground then hover for a moment and then make your final descent towards touchdown. Again, this should be slow.

Gently Touch Down

Bring the helicopter down very slow so that when you touch down the helicopter just rests on the landing skids. Do not bounce the copter when landing. Just set it down as easily as possible.

If at any time in the landing process something should not go right, or if you feel something is happening too fast, **gently** give it more power to rise it up a little bit and start the process over again. It is better to take a couple of tries to make a nice and gentle landing than it is to make one try and crash.

Slowly Stop Rotors

Slow down the rotors gradually. Trying to stop them too quickly might cause the copter to tilt and hit the blades on the ground.

The spinning blades have some inertia in them and this can cause problems if you try to stop too quickly. Like everything else, slow the blades down easily.

Do not approach the helicopter or try to pick it up until the blades totally stop spinning. Some of the larger blades can cause some pretty nasty cuts or worse.

Naturally, and this goes without saying, NEVER try and catch a helicopter or land it in your hands. Those blades can be real nasty when they are spinning.

Learning How to Fly Your Helicopter

Now that you have mastered the basics and can get your helicopter to stay in one place hovering a few inches or so off the ground, it is time to get a little more daring and a little more complicated. But let's just make sure you have done everything in part one and are comfortable with everything. If you are not, stop and go back to the exercises in part one. These skills are critical to keep your copter in the air and minimize crashes and damage. Do NOT go on until you feel confident!

Step One: Controlling Your Copter

Speed and height are worth nothing unless you can control where your helicopter goes and how it gets to where it is going. If you can't control it, you will crash it or lose it!

Mark off an area about 15 feet by 20 feet for most mid-sized helicopters and larger for the big boys!

Practice hovering and landing your helicopter inside this area. Make smaller boxes and practice taking off from one box and landing in another. Always keep the helicopter within the marked off area.

Fly it around the edges making turns at the corners. Speed is not important, control is. If you have a two blade copter this will be easier but the larger helicopters with a tail rotor will be more difficult. Keep practicing until you can turn and control the helicopter and land in the boxes. Do this for at least two full battery packs. You should get so that everything becomes a habit and you can do it pretty much without thinking.

Step Two: More Control of Your Copter!

When you are comfortable flying forward within the box, try flying in reverse. Remember that flying in reverse means that some of the control will work backwards as well. Get used to flying forwards and backwards. There will be times in flight when you will have to fly backwards to get away from an obstacle or other object. Better to learn here than up there when that happens!

Step Three: Turns Moving Forward

Now it's time to make wider turns while moving forward. That means turning the copter while it is moving forward or in reverse.

This will take some co-ordination between hands on your controller but it is not hard once you get the hang of it.

Step Four: Let Me Take You Higher!

Repeat the exercises we have talked about with your copter higher in the air. Try it about 3 ft off the ground, then 5 ft and higher. Always wait until you are comfortable at a certain height before going higher. Remember the higher you go the more damage a crash will bring. Take it slow.

Also keep in mind that the higher you go the more wind will become a factor. Wind will move your copter around and you need to be able to compensate for this with turns and speed.

Step Five: Longer Distance Flights

As you get comfortable with higher flight heights, you also need to get used to flying the copter further away from you. You need to get used to watching the copter as it gets smaller and still understanding where it is and how to get it where you want it.

This takes time and patience and experience. Do not rush this and force yourself. Remember this is supposed to be relaxing and fun! Some people are happy with small local flights and never fly it far from where they are. Others like to test the limits of the controller and go higher and farther. Neither is wrong, it is a personal preference.

Remember the controls will act differently when the copter is moving away from you than they do when the copter is moving towards you.

Turn controls will act the reverse way and you need to realize and understand this. Again, this comes with experience and patience.

All Steps: Easy Does It!

The controls used in flying helicopters are very sensitive. Make all movements slow and deliberate and do not do fast or violent actions. Speed should be gradually increased to raise the copter and gradually lowered to bring the copter down.

One common action is to dramatically reduce rotor speed when something unexpected happens. The result is a copter that is plummeting to the ground heading for a crash. Always bring the copter down slowly for a controlled descent to minimize damage and to land in a safe manner.

The faster the copter is moving the more sensitive the controls are likely to be. Because of this, take your time in getting used to the controls and their effects as you go faster and higher. Eventually you will get the "hang" of it and be able to control your radio controlled helicopter like a pro.

There is something I feel I must address because it has caused some confusion in earlier versions of this book. While we stress the "easy does it" approach to flying, you should do what works for your particular type of aircraft.

If too gradual movements cause your helicopter to fall over on take off, you might have to be a tad more agressive. But as a rule, gradual and controlled movements of the joystick or transmitter will produce more stable and controlled flight.

The Keys to flight Success!

1) Take it slow and do not proceed to the next step before you are comfortable with the preceding step. Each step is important to learn and master. If you give yourself time you will become a much better pilot!

2) Take it slow! Slow ascent (rise) and a slow controlled descent (landing) is the best way to minimize damage and control movements.

3) Become comfortable with all actions and maneuvers at lower heights before going higher.

4) Read your manual and follow their directions. They know best!

5) Always do a pre-flight checklist and fly only in suitable weather.

Avoiding a Crash!

There will be times when you will crash. It happens to everyone. That does not mean that there is nothing we can do to control how often it happens because we can. But to say we can avoid all crashes is just not realistic.

Crashes occur for one of three reasons. Those reasons are pilot error, equipment malfunction and environmental reasons. We can influence all three causes of crashes and reduce the chances of crashing if we take a few simple precautions.

Here are a few things to consider and do when it comes to minimizing crashes:

Practice, Practice, Practice

Most crashes are due to pilot error and the majority of those occur when people get nervous or panic. This happens because the pilot is not yet comfortable or experienced enough to handle adversity or pressure when it arrives.

There are two ways or getting experience. You can get it on a flight simulator which is a risk free and easy way to learn. Or, you can get it by flying your aircraft and experiencing thing first hand. This is a lot riskier but you still have to actually fly at some point.

If you want to get real life experience it really helps if you have someone who knows how to fly standing with you. This could be a friend or you could join a club and fly with other pilots. This way if you get into trouble you can hand off the controller and the experienced pilot can recover and stabilize the aircraft and return the controller to you. Then you two can discuss what happened and what should have been done differently.

Pilot error is going to happen until you get enough experience to where everything is done from memory and without too much thinking. You see something happen and your hands just react automatically. This is when you know you have arrived as a pilot. For some this can take a few flights while others might take a lot longer. The type and quality of the aircraft will also be a factor. That is why we suggested a trainer aircraft for the new pilot.

Last, but certainly not least, is that most pilot error consists of making large control movements instead of smaller ones. Nervousness and inexperience are almost always the cause for this. Remember to make small and controlled movements and to monitor each movement and its effect. Then adjust and control as needed. Small and controlled is always better than large and abrupt movements.

Fly Within Yourself

You should always fly within your skills. Granted you need to improve and that comes from pushing yourself a little every time out but we should not be un-boxing our aircraft for the first time and trying to do loops and barrel rolls! Become comfortable with the basics until you can do them almost without thinking. Then you can advance and try something new.

Fly at an altitude that will give you the best chance at recovery. In the beginning that will mean flying higher because it will take you longer to recover. But as you gain experience you will recover faster and can safely fly lower.

The same goes for your choice of aircraft. Do not start out with a complicated and hard to fly $2,000 aircraft. Go with an easy to fly trainer and learn on that. There is plenty of time to improve and trade up to larger and more sophisticated aircraft.

Perform Maintenance

You can have all the pilot skills in the world but if you send up a damaged or broken aircraft you greatly increase your chances of crashing. Check and tighten all connections and linkages. Check batteries for charge and leakage or other problems. Check the body for damage and to make sure all flight control surfaces operate as they should.

Follow you instruction manual for recommended maintenance and follow those instructions to the letter. Do not skimp on maintenance. It may not be glamorous and it might not be fun but it will save you money and heartache in the future.

Do Pre-Flight Checks

Even though you did maintenance, always check everything before taking off. Check the operation of all flight surfaces and make sure everything works smooth and without strange or unusual noises. If something doesn't look or sound right, check it out before taking off.

When you do take off, fly your aircraft through a little test pattern to make sure it behaves like it should. If it does then go on and fly however you want to. But if something seems odd or wrong, then land and check it out.

Be Aware of Your Environment

When you get to the flight area, take a look around and take note of trees, buildings, power lines and other obstacles that can influence your flight. Power lines and aircraft do not really get along well together and you should do your best to stay away from them. It doesn't take a great pilot to fly through power lines, it takes a stupid pilot. Stay away from them!

Always know which way the wind is blowing and how strong it is. Don't go up on windy days especially if you are flying a trainer or very light aircraft.

That is just itching for trouble. Also be aware that it might be calm on the ground but windy and gusty 100-200 feet up. If you start to see your aircraft being blown all over, reduce altitude until it becomes more stable or land altogether.

So make sure no one else is flying their aircraft on your frequency. Don't rely on other people to check even if you are there first. Some pilots don't care about anyone other than themselves. Make it your responsibility to check with anyone else that is flying. It doesn't cost any more of less to fix your aircraft if someone else is the cause of the crash.

Take Responsibility

This might seem a little odd but you will have better results when it comes to flying your RC aircraft if you just take total responsibility for everything that happens. It might be easier to blame someone else for not doing this or for causing that but the ultimate focus needs to be on preventing problems than assessing who was to blame.

If you take responsibility the chances of you properly maintaining your aircraft and checking out your environment will be far better than if you constantly blame someone else. When we take responsibility for the things we do then we learn from our mistakes.

But if we do something wrong and convince ourselves that something or someone else was to blame, we probably will continue to make those same mistakes over and over again. That might mean crashing over and over and over again as well.

Do the things you should, make the right decisions and use the control in the right way and you should minimize the chances of crashing every time you go out. But we cannot control the unexpected gust of wind or the midair controller failure. Those are part of RC flying and we just need to embrace that and deal with it.

Just take responsibility for the things under your control and you will do just fine in this great hobby.

When You Crash!

Crash is a word that RC flyers have feared since day one. But it is a word that refers to something everyone who purchasing an RC aircraft eventually will do. That's right, everyone eventually crashes. While there are a lot of things we can do to minimize the chances of us crashing there is absolutely nothing we can do to guarantee that we will not crash.

So just deal with it!

There are so many reasons for crashes that it just is not possible to cover all the bases and make yourself 100% bulletproof. Instead, we need to focus on doing the right thing when we crash to minimize the impact and the cost of those crashes.

First of all, try not to get upset when you crash. Remember everyone crashes from beginners to seasoned pros that have been flying for decades. You are not special or unique and I seriously doubt if you were the first person to do whatever you did that caused the crash.

If, in fact, it was something you did. This is one time in life where it is comforting not to be unique or special.

All that being said, there are some things you can do when the inevitable times draws close. Here are some tips to get you through a crash with minimum impact:

Find a Soft Spot to Crash

Though this might sound a little stupid, sometimes we have some warning and the time to not avoid a crash but direct the aircraft in a specific direction. For example you lost engine control but you can still turn.

In those cases try and get your plane over a softer area like loose dirt or sand. Stay away from a parking lot of concrete. Stay away from trees which love to eat planes in their branches. The last thing you want to do for the next 6 months is see your plane stuck 100 feet up in the tree! In other words, try and direct the aircraft over an area where impact will do the least amount of harm.

Get to the Spot Quickly

Don't waste time yelling and pouting and standing there. Get to the spot quickly so you can see what happened and take immediate action. If it is a gas plane it might have caught fire and getting their quickly might not only save parts of the aircraft but the surrounding area as well.

But the most important reason for getting there quickly is to make sure no one was hurt or injured during the crash.

Spinning propellers can cause deep cuts if the plane should fly into anyone, especially a child. Get to where the aircraft went down as quickly as possible and make sure everything else is OK. Then go to your aircraft.

Another reason to get their first is that others in the area are likely to be drawn to the crash and curiosity will take over. You don't want people touching your aircraft, taking pieces of it home with them, or getting cut or injured playing with it.

Survey the Area

When you get to the crash area, take a quick look around to see if you see any parts of the aircraft scattered around. If you flew in at an angle wings might have broken off 30 or 4 yards away. So look all around to see where parts and pieces might be. Helicopters, on the other hand, tend to fall down fairly straight so wreckage will not be as scattered.

Another thing to consider is whether or not parts broke off in flight and that was the cause of the crash. If that was the case, try and figure out where those parts fell. Who knows you might just be able to find them and epoxy them back on and save the aircraft,

Carry a Plastic Bag with You

Some crashes will involve little wreckage and some minor physical damage. In fact, most crashes are in that category.

But other crashes will have significant damage and several detached parts. It might be difficult to carry all those parts so having a plastic bag to place the parts as you see them will come in very handy. Keep the bag in your tool bag or box so it will be there when you need it.

Evaluate and Repair

When you crash you need to be able to evaluate the damage and determine if it is something you can fix or if others might have to do the work. Or whether it is repairable at all.

Whether or not to repair a damaged plane will depend on the costs involved and the overall damage. If a $100 aircraft needs $200 worth of repairs, you should just purchase another aircraft. But if you are doing the work and your only investment is time and some glue, then you have to place a value on your time and make the decision.

You also need to understand that repairs have to be much more than cosmetic. You can repair an airplane to look perfect but if the materials you used cause one side to weight more than the other it will not fly right. So repairs not only have to look good, they must fly well and be strong as well.

This requires a certain number of skills that not everyone possesses. Please be honest before you invest a lot of time and money into something you might not be able to do.

Conclusion

Today is a great time to be involved in flying Electric RC aircraft. Technology has given us lighter, smaller and more full featured models than ever before. And things will only get better as technology further moves forward.

But this hobby is not about having the best or latest aircraft or who can fly the highest or fastest. It is all about who is having fun and who is just enjoying themselves the most. Having fun and enjoying ourselves is the best reason for doing anything and RC flying is no different.

For that reason, try and enjoy the entire process. From researching your first plane to learning how to assemble it and get it into the air everything should be fun. You should enjoy maintaining it and tinkering with it and making each plane your own.

Don't rush through any part of the experience. To do that might mean making the wrong decision or buying the wrong plane or just spending more than what you should. Take the time to enjoy the entire process. You will be glad you did.

This hobby is also about staying within your skills and comfort zone. While it is OK, and even good, to want to improve your skills, it is not necessary to take on tasks for which you receive no joy or excitement.

That means you do not need to build your own plane in order to love flying. Just because some people do, many others do not. I, for example, built one plane and enjoyed the process but have no desire to do it again. To each their own, I guess. The only thing that matters is who has the most fun.

This is also a hobby that lends itself to participating with others such as in clubs or just by yourself on a nice Saturday afternoon. Whatever your choice might be, just go out and enjoy flying your RC aircraft. That is the entire point of the hobby.

I would also like to ask you to be a considerate RC pilot. Don't give the entire hobby a bad reputation by flying in a dangerous or irresponsible manner or by interrupting people at 7AM on a Sunday morning. Be considerate of others and enjoy yourself at the same time.

I would like to say that this is a great way to spend time with your children. It is exciting to not only watch your aircraft flying around but to also see the joy and wonder on your children's faces at the same time. That only adds to the overall fun and enjoyment.

So go out and have a great time with your Electric RC aircraft.

We hope the material in this book will help you not only have more fun but also make the journey a pleasant and informative one as well.

Happy Flying!

PS. If you liked this book, could you please take a moment and give us a positive review on Amazon? This will help others who are looking to get into this great hobby be aware that this book might help them as well.
Thanks!

FREE R/C Hobby Information!

We would like to thank you for purchasing this book on radio controlled helicopters. To show our appreciation, we would like to send you a free report with some more information on R/C hobbying that will help you get more enjoyment from this great hobby.

There is no obligation on your part to get this free report. Just click on the link below, or copy and paste it into your web browser to access the webpage. It's our way of saying thank you and helping you get even more from your R/C experience!

http://www.howtomastery.com/radiocontrolled.html

Printed in Great
Britain
by Amazon